T0211838

Lecture Notes in Computer Science　12285

More information about this series at http://www.springer.com/series/7407

Zhicheng Dou · Qiguang Miao ·
Wei Lu · Jiaxin Mao · Guang Jia (Eds.)

Information Retrieval

26th China Conference, CCIR 2020
Xi'an, China, August 14–16, 2020
Proceedings

 Springer

Editors
Zhicheng Dou
Renmin University of China
Beijing, China

Qiguang Miao
Xidian University
Xi'an, Shaanxi, China

Wei Lu
Wuhan University
Wuhan, Hubei, China

Jiaxin Mao
Tsinghua University
Beijing, China

Guang Jia
Xidian University
Xi'an, Shaanxi, China

ISSN 0302-9743   ISSN 1611-3349   (electronic)
Lecture Notes in Computer Science
ISBN 978-3-030-56724-8   ISBN 978-3-030-56725-5   (eBook)
https://doi.org/10.1007/978-3-030-56725-5

LNCS Sublibrary: SL1 – Theoretical Computer Science and General Issues

This Springer imprint is published by the registered company Springer Nature Switzerland AG
The registered company address is: Gewerbestrasse 11, 6330 Cham, Switzerland

Preface

The China Conference on Information Retrieval (CCIR 2020), co-organized by the Chinese Computer Federation (CCF) and the Chinese Information Processing Society of China (CIPS), was the 26th installment of the conference series. The conference was hosted by Xidian University in Xi'an, Shaanxi, China, during August 14–16, 2020. Due to the COVID-19 pandemic, instead of being held as an on-site conference, CCIR 2020 was an online conference supplemented with local on-site events in some Chinese cities.

The annual CCIR conference serves as the major forum for researchers and practitioners from both China and other Asian countries/regions to share their ideas, present new research results, and demonstrate new systems and techniques in the broad field of information retrieval (IR). Since CCIR 2017, the conference has enjoyed contributions spanning the theory and application of IR, both in English and Chinese. This year we received a total of 102 submissions from both China and other Asian countries. Each submission was carefully reviewed by at least three domain experts, and the Program Committee (PC) chairs made the final decision. We accepted 62, among which 12 were English papers and 50 were Chinese papers. The final English program of CCIR 2020 featured 12 papers.

CCIR 2020 included abundant academic activities. Besides keynote speeches delivered by world-renowned scientists from China and abroad, as well as traditional paper presentation sessions and poster sessions, we also hosted a young scientist forum, an evaluation workshop, and tutorials on frontier research topics. We also invited authors in related international conferences (such as SIGIR and CIKM) to share their research results as well. CCIR 2020 featured four keynote speeches by Jun Yan (YiduCloud), Xing Xie (Microsoft Research Asia), Qiang Yang (HKUST, Webank) and Xiaochuan Wang (Sogou Inc.).

The conference and program chairs of CCIR 2020 extend their sincere gratitude to all authors and contributors to this year's conference. We are also grateful to the PC members for their reviewing effort, which guaranteed that CCIR 2020 could feature a quality program of original and innovative research in IR. Special thanks go to our sponsors for their generosity: Microsoft STCA (Software Technology Center Asia) and Gaoling School of Artificial Intelligence, Renmin University of China.

August 2020

Xinbo Gao
Xueqi Cheng
Zhicheng Dou
Qiguang Miao
Wei Lu
Jiaxin Mao
Guang Jia

Organization

General Chairs

Xinbo Gao   Xidian University, China
Xueqi Cheng   Institute of Computing Technology, Chinese Academy
                                 of Sciences, China

Program Committee Chairs

Zhicheng Dou   Renmin University of China, China
Qiguang Miao   Xidian University, China
Wei Lu   Wuhan University, China

Publicity Chair

Jiali Zuo   Jiangxi Normal University, China

Proceedings Chairs

Jiaxin Mao   Tsinghua University, China
Guang Jia   Xidian University, China

Webmaster

Peiyi Shen   Xidian University, China

Youth Forum Chairs

Min Zhang   Tsinghua University, China
Xiangnan He   University of Science and Technology of China, China

CCIR Cup Chairs

Liqiang Nie   Shandong University, China
Xiaofei Zhu   Chongqing University of Technology, China

Sponsorship Chairs

Jun Xu   Renmin University of China, China
Daxin Jiang   Microsoft Software Technology Center Asia

Treasurer

Jianfeng Song   Xidian University, China

Summer School Chairs

Yanyan Lan   Institute of Computing Technology, Chinese Academy
                             of Sciences, China
Ruyi Liu   Xidian University, China

Award Chair

Tie-Yan Liu   Microsoft Research Asia

Program Committee

Ting Bai   Beijing University of Posts and Telecommunications,
                             China
Yubo Chen   Institute of Automation, Chinese Academy of Sciences,
                             China
Zhumin Chen   Shandong University, China
Shoubin Dong   South China University of Technology, China
Jiafeng Guo   Institute of Computing Technology, Chinese Academy
                             of Sciences, China
Zhongyuan Han   Harbin Institute of Technology, China
Yu Hong   Soochow University, China
Xuanjing Huang   Fudan University, China
Feng Ji   DAMO Academy, Alibaba Group, China
Ting Jin   Hainan University, China
Xiaolong Jin   Institute of Computing Technology, Chinese Academy
                             of Sciences, China
Yanyan Lan   Institute of Computing Technology, Chinese Academy
                             of Sciences, China
Chenliang Li   Wuhan University, China
Ru Li   Shanxi University, China
Zhi Li   Guangxi Normal University, China
Hongfei Lin   Dalian University of Technology, China
Yuan Lin   Dalian University of Technology, China
Chang Liu   Peking University, China
Kang Liu   Institute of Automation, Chinese Academy of Sciences,
                             China
Peiyu Liu   Shandong Normal University, China
Shenghua Liu   Institute of Computing Technology, Chinese Academy
                             of Sciences, China
Tie-Yan Liu   Microsoft Research Asia
Yiqun Liu   Tsinghua University, China

Yue Liu	Institute of Computing Technology, Chinese Academy of Sciences, China
Cheng Luo	Tsinghua University, China
Zhunchen Luo	PLA Academy of Military Science, China
Jianming Lv	South China University of Technology, China
Jun Ma	Shandong University, China
Weizhi Ma	Tsinghua University, China
Jiaxin Mao	Tsinghua University, China
Xian-Ling Mao	Beijing Institute of Technology, China
Liang Pang	Institute of Automation, Chinese Academy of Sciences, China
Zhaochun Ren	Shandong University, China
Tong Ruan	East China University of Science and Technology, China
Huawei Shen	Institute of Computing Technology, Chinese Academy of Sciences, China
Mingwen Wang	Jiangxi Normal University, China
Pengfei Wang	Beijing University of Posts and Telecommunications, China
Ji-Rong Wen	Renmin University of China, China
Long Xia	York University, Canada
Xiangwen Liao	Fuzhou University, China
Tong Xiao	Northeastern University, China
Jun Xu	Renmin University of China, China
Ruifeng Xu	Harbin Institute of Technology, China
Tong Xu	University of Science and Technology of China, China
Weiran Xu	Beijing University of Posts and Telecommunications, China
Hongfei Yan	Peking University, China
Zhihao Yang	Dalian University of Technology, China
Zhang Yu	Harbin Institute of Technology, China
Chengzhi Zhang	Nanjing University of Science and Technology, China
Min Zhang	Tsinghua University, China
Qi Zhang	Fudan University, China
Ying Zhang	Nankai University, China
Xin Zhao	Renmin University of China, China
Jianxing Zheng	Shanxi University, China
Jianke Zhu	Zhejiang University, China
Xiaofei Zhu	Chongqing University of Technology, China
Zhenfang Zhu	Shandong Jiaotong University, China
Jiali Zuo	Jiangxi Normal University, China

Contents

Search and Recommendation

Improving Search Snippets
in Context-Aware Web Search Scenarios

Jia Chen, Jiaxin Mao, Yiqun Liu$^{(\boxtimes)}$, Min Zhang, and Shaoping Ma

Department of Computer Science and Technology, Institute for Artificial Intelligence,
Beijing National Research Center for Information Science and Technology,
Tsinghua University, Beijing 100084, China
chenjia0831@gmail.com, maojiaxin@gmail.com,
{yiqunliu,z-m,msp}@tsinghua.edu.cn

Abstract. As an essential part in web search, search snippets usually
provide result previews for users to either gather useful information or
make click-through decisions. In complex search scenarios, users may
need to submit multiple queries to search systems until their information needs are satisfied. As user intents tend to be ambiguous, incorporating contextual information for user modeling has been proved effective
in many session-level tasks. Therefore, the generation of search snippets may also benefit from the integration of context information. However, to our best knowledge, most existing snippet generation methods
ignore user interaction and focus merely on the query content. Whether
it is useful of exploiting session contexts to improve search snippets still
remains inscrutable. To this end, we propose a snippet generation model
which considers session contexts. The proposed method utilizes the query
sequence as well as users' interaction behaviors within a session to model
users' session-level information needs. We also adopt practical log-based
search data to evaluate the performance of the proposed method. Experiment results based on both expert annotation and user preference test
show the effectiveness of considering contextual information in search
snippet generation.

Keywords: Search snippets · User intent · Web search

1 Introduction

Snippets are an essential part in Search Engine Result Pages (SERPs). A search
engine analyzes the content or metadata of a webpage and then extracts a small
clip, i.e., a snippet, to help search users preview the landing page. Before clicking
on a certain result, the user can only learn about the result content by its title
or snippet. However, result titles are generally short and simple, usually directly
citing the titles of corresponding webpages. Moreover, some of them contain

This work is supported by Natural Science Foundation of China (Grant No. 61622208,
61532011, 61672311) and National Key Basic Research Program (2015CB358700).

Z. Dou et al. (Eds.): CCIR 2020, LNCS 12285, pp. 3–16, 2020.
https://doi.org/10.1007/978-3-030-56725-5_1

exaggerated or mendacious information, a.k.a. the *clickbaits* [17], which may lure users into clicking. In this scenario, search snippets are more credible for users to gain useful information and could be therefore essential for improving users' satisfaction.

Snippets may play a more important role in complex search scenarios e.g., exploratory search. A user may not have a clear information need at the beginning. She needs to submit a few queries and interacts with some results to learn about the search task. In this scenario, she can obtain relevant information in the snippets and acquire effective query terms from them to reformulate her next query [9]. Sometimes query content may not fully reflect users' information needs, thus contextual information such as query history or clickthrough data should be exploited. However, query-biased snippets [6,7] are dominating in most commercial search engines nowadays. They are usually generated in the manner of selecting several relevant sentences in the result document. Few of them take the session contexts into consideration. Some previous studies propose to use pseudo or implicit relevance feedback to optimize the snippet generation [7,8]. These methods utilize the text statistics in the whole corpus rather than the contextual information within a session. Therefore, they may not successfully capture user intent in the current search tasks.

To address this issue, we propose a model to generate context-aware search snippets. Previous studies have shown great advantages of considering search contexts for session-level IR tasks. Inspired by [1], we adopt the *feedback memory mechanism* to encode session contexts. The mechanism represents users' session-level information needs based on the positive and negative feedbacks derived from their interactions. Based on the session-level representation, the model can rate each sentence in a candidate document with a relevance score. Then by considering different traits of good snippets, we design multiple methods to integrate the context-aware relevance scores into snippet generation and further evaluate their performances, respectively.

To summarize, the main contributions of our work are as follows:

- We present a novel extractive method which considers session contexts for context-aware search snippet generation.
- Experiment results based on both intrinsic and extrinsic evaluation validate mutually and indicate the effectiveness of the proposed model.

2   Related Work

2.1   Snippet Generation

Without loss of generality, snippet generation can be broadly categorized into two classes: *extractive summarization* and *abstractive summarization*. Extractive methods usually include analyzing the result page, selecting appropriate text content or media, and then forming a concise snippet to display on the SERP. Besides extracting sentences from a webpage, *paraphrasing* its content, a.k.a. abstractive summarization, is also available. Mainstream commercial search engines usually adopt extractive methods due to the high cost of generating high-quality sentences for billions of result pages. Therefore, we do not consider abstractive methods for search snippet generation in this paper.

Numerous work have focused on extractive snippets generation. For example, Wang et al. [5] propose a *query-biased* webpage summarization method which introduces a scheme to rank candidate sentences in the result. Some other studies consider using user feedbacks to optimize snippet generation [7], e.g., Ko et al. [7] apply pseudo-relevance feedbacks and text summarization techniques to extract salient sentences for generating high-quality snippets. However, they utilize query contents as pseudo feedbacks and ignore user interactions. To better model user search intent, Ageev et al. [22] incorporate user mouse movement signals to learn *behavior-biased* snippets and open a new direction for improving search result presentation.

2.2 Snippet Evaluation

So far no standard metrics have been designed for search snippet evaluation. Therefore, NLG-summarization evaluation approaches are widely adopted. On one hand, some studies conduct snippet evaluation with *intrinsic* methods, that is, evaluating generated summaries by manually comparing them with human-created ones [12]. As factitious comparison is time-consuming, many evaluation agencies such as the Document Understanding Conference (DUC) adopt ROUGE [4] to access the quality of generated texts. The main idea of ROUGE is to compare the basic syntactic units (e.g. n-grams, word sequences, ordered pairs) with standard summaries generated by human experts and count the number of the overlapped ones. In our experiments, we also use ROUGE to evaluate the quality of the generated snippets.

Although *intrinsic* methods are convenient for evaluation, they lack user perception. Therefore, *extrinsic* evaluation with users involved is necessary. The core idea of extrinsic summarization evaluation is to determine the effect of summaries based on human perception tasks. For instance, one can examine the usefulness or the satisfaction of a snippet/summary with respect to her information needs or goals [13]. From this perspective, we conduct a user preference test to collect their preference on the paired snippets.

3 Extractive Context-Aware Snippet Generation

In this section, we propose a context-aware snippet generation model based on the *feedback memory mechanism*. We start by elaborating how it encodes user information needs and preferences within a search session, and then introduce how to generate context-aware snippets based on session-level representations.

3.1 User Preference Modeling

To model session-level user intents, we adopt the feedback memory mechanism to represent the session context. As shown in Fig. 1, users' interactions are taken as inputs and will be converted into distributed representations. We further use encoding layers and attention mechanisms to embed user positive/negative feedbacks. Finally, we feed the feedback embeddings as well as the query representations into a recurrent neural network to represent the whole search session.

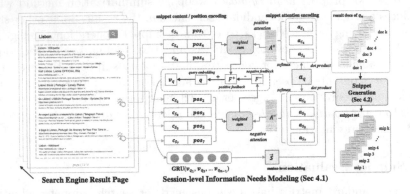

Fig. 1. Main framework of our model. Here shows an example of using clicked (1, 4, 6) and skipped (2, 3, 5, 7) snippets as the positive and negative feedbacks.

Positive/Negative Feedback Snippets. Here we collect user behaviors on each result snippet as the feedback signals. We use clicks as positive feedbacks and skips as negative ones. According to the cascade assumption [14], a user scans the result list from top to bottom and examines the result right after the last clicked one to determine whether to end this query session. Therefore, we consider all the unclicked result which rank higher or just one position lower than the last clicked result as skipped results. For a given query q and its result documents $\mathcal{D} = \{d_1, ...d_i, ...d_n\}$, the positive/negative feedback snippets $\mathcal{S}^+/\mathcal{S}^-$ can be represented as $\mathcal{S}^+ = \{\mathcal{S}_p | p \in \mathcal{C}\}, \mathcal{S}^- = \{\mathcal{S}_p | p \leq max(\mathcal{C}) + 1, p \notin \mathcal{C}\}$, where $\mathcal{S}_p$ denotes the snippet content of d_p, and $\mathcal{C}$ is the set that contains the positions of all the clicked documents. The whole framework consists of a snippet content encoding layer, a position encoding layer, and an attention layer to represent the positive/negative feedback memory $\mathcal{F}^+/\mathcal{F}^-$. These three components will be introduced in the next, respectively.

Snippet Content Encoding and Position Encoding. A snippet is regarded as a sequence of words it contains $\mathcal{S}_p = \{x_1^p, ...x_j^p ..., x_{|\mathcal{S}_p|}^p\}$. We apply the standard **G**ated **R**ecurrent **U**nits (GRUs) [15] to encode a snippet into a fixed size vector:

$$\mathbf{w}_j^p = \mathbf{E}_c^T \cdot \mathbf{x}_j^p, \tag{1}$$

$$\mathbf{c}_{\mathcal{S}_p} = \text{GRU}_c(\mathbf{w}_1^p, ..., \mathbf{w}_j^p ..., \mathbf{w}_{|\mathcal{S}_p|}^p), \tag{2}$$

here $\mathbf{E}_c \in \mathbb{R}^{V \times l}$ is the word embedding matrix, $\mathbf{x}_j^p$ and $\mathbf{w}_j^p \in \mathbb{R}^V$ represent the one-hot vector and the distributed vector (embedding) for the j-th word of the snippet at position p, respectively. V is the vocabulary size and l is the dimension of word embeddings. $\mathbf{c}_{\mathcal{S}_p}$ is the output of the last hidden layer state in GRU, which represents the content of a snippet.

The position of a snippet also influences users' perception of its relevance to a certain extent, hence we encode the ranking position of snippets by $\mathbf{pos}_p = \mathbf{E}_{pos}^T \cdot \mathbf{p}$, where $\mathbf{E}_{pos}$ is the learnable embedding matrix for all ranking positions and $\mathbf{p}$ denotes the one-hot presentation for position p. In this paper, we only consider the top 15 results for a query.

Attention Mechanism. We combine the text embedding and position embedding of a snippet with an attention mechanism and use the weighted combinations as the positive/negative feedback memory $\mathcal{F}^+/\mathcal{F}^-$. For a specific query, we learn the positive attention $\mathcal{A}^+$ and the negative attention $\mathcal{A}^-$ separately. For a query $q = \{x_1^q, ...x_j^q, ..., x_{|q|}^q\}$ and a snippet $\mathcal{S}_p = \{x_1^p, ...x_j^p ..., x_{|\mathcal{S}_p|}^p\}$, we also embed the words first and then use GRUs to encode them into two fixed-length vectors $\mathbf{a}_q$ and $\mathbf{a}_{\mathcal{S}_p}$ respectively:

$$\mathbf{w}_j^q = \mathbf{E}_q^T \cdot \mathbf{x}_j^q, \tag{3}$$

$$\mathbf{w}_j^p = \mathbf{E}_{a_\mathcal{S}}^T \cdot \mathbf{x}_j^p, \tag{4}$$

$$\mathbf{a}_q = \mathrm{GRU}_q(\mathbf{w}_1^q, ..., \mathbf{w}_j^q ..., \mathbf{w}_{|q|}^q), \tag{5}$$

$$\mathbf{a}_{\mathcal{S}_p} = \mathrm{GRU}_{a_\mathcal{S}}(\mathbf{w}_1^p, ..., \mathbf{w}_j^p ..., \mathbf{w}_{|\mathcal{S}_p|}^p). \tag{6}$$

The attention distribution of a query q on a snippet is given by the dot product of these two vectors. We can represent the positive or negative attention $\mathcal{A}^+/\mathcal{A}^-$ with *softmax* function over positive or feedback snippets $\mathcal{S}^+/\mathcal{S}^-$: $\mathcal{A}_\mathcal{S}^{+/-} = softmax(\mathbf{a}_q^T \mathbf{a}_{\mathcal{S}_p} | \mathcal{S}_p \in \mathcal{S}^{+/-})$.

Feedback Memory Mechanism. We then concatenate the snippet content embeddings and position embeddings together and feed them into a dense layer. The output vectors of this layer will be weighted by the attention distribution to calculate the feedback memory:

$$\mathcal{F}^{+/-} = \sum_{\mathcal{S}_p \in \mathcal{S}^{+/-}} \mathcal{A}_\mathcal{S}^{+/-}(\mathbf{W}[\mathbf{c}_{\mathcal{S}_p} \oplus \mathbf{pos}_p] + \mathbf{b}_F), \tag{7}$$

where $\mathcal{F}^+$ and $\mathcal{F}^-$ represent users' positive preferences and negative preferences within the session, respectively. $\mathbf{W}$ and $\mathbf{b}_F$ are the weight matrix and the bias of the dense layer. "$\oplus$" denotes the vector concatenation.

Session-Level Embedding. As the output $\mathcal{F}^+/\mathcal{F}^-$ capture user preference on a query, we further utilize it to present the session-level contexts. We first combine the query embeddings with feedback memories and then feed the combined vectors into a session-level GRU:

$$\mathbf{v}_{q_k} = \mathbf{q}_k + \mathcal{F}^+ - \mathcal{F}^-, \tag{8}$$

$$\mathbf{S} = \mathrm{GRU}_s(\mathbf{v}_{q_1}, ... \mathbf{v}_{q_k}, ... \mathbf{v}_{q_K}). \tag{9}$$

Training Objective Function. The entire architecture is trained end-to-end[1]. Here we select the log-likelihood of decoding the last query $q_s = \{x_1, ...x_j, ..., x_{|q_s|}\}$

---

[1] For all datasets, we train the network for 200 epochs because the training losses have converged stably within 200 epochs.

within the session from the session representation **S** as the objective function. For lack of golden context-aware snippets for each result, the last query is used as a surrogate training target because it implies a user's current search intention. This training function can be formulated as follows:

$$\log \mathcal{L}(M) = \sum_{x_j \in q_s} \log P_M(x_j | x_1 : x_{j-1}, \mathbf{S}). \tag{10}$$

3.2   Snippet Generation

Candidate Scoring. After training, we use Eq. 11 to assign a relevance score for each candidate sentence. For a sentence $s = \{x_1, ...x_j, ..., x_{|s|}\}$, the score is represented as the probability of decoding a sentence from a given session-level representation S:

$$score(s) = \prod_{j, x_j \in s} P(x_j | x_1 : x_{j-1}, S). \tag{11}$$

Then we can design various snippet generation approaches based on these scores.

Simple Sorting (SS). A simple method is to directly rank the sentences by their relevance scores in the descending order and select those with the highest relevance scores. The process of Simple Sorting can be formulated as:

$$Snippet_{ss} = \arg\max_{\Omega'} \sum_{s \in \Omega'} S_{ss}(s), \ s.t. \sum_{s \in \Omega'} |s| \leq L, s \in \Omega, \tag{12}$$

$$S_{ss}(s) = score(s) + \sum_{i=1, x_i \in q_s}^{n} N(x_i) \cdot TFIDF(x_i), \tag{13}$$

where $S_{ss}(s)$ denotes the score of a sentence s, x_i is the i-th word in the query q_s, $N(x)$ represents the appearance number of a query word x in the sentence s, Ω is the set of candidate sentences, Ω' represents the selected sentences, and L is the word limit for a snippet. According to previous work [3], the length of a snippet has a great impact on the snippet quality. So we strictly unify the lengths of all the generated snippets.

N-tuple Sorting (NS). Snippets should be understandable and readable. So far it is unknown whether a single sentence could convey clear and integrated ideas to readers. Therefore, we cut each document into n-sentence subsequences and then rank them according to their summed scores in Eq. 13. Due to the word limit, we only consider the case of $n = 2, 3$ here.

Diversified Sorting (DS). To avoid redundancy, we try to increase the diversity of snippets by the Maximal Marginal Relevance (MMR) [16] of candidate sentences. We first select the sentence with the highest Simple Sorting score and then sequentially choose sentences with the highest marginal relevance score S_{ds} in the remaining candidate set until exceeding the word limit. The marginal relevance score S_{ds} is defined as follows:

Table 1. Statistics for each dataset.

Specific\Dataset	SD_1	SD_2	SQE	UPT
# sessions	115	246	200	99
# queries	486	795	727	358
# top15 web pages	18,244	51,042	–	–
# pages for annotation	–	–	632	880

⋆ Note that SQE is short for the dataset used in Snippet Quality Evaluation (Sect. 4.2) and UPT is short for the dataset used in User Preference Test (Sect. 4.3)

$$S_{ds}(s_i^t) = \beta \cdot S_{ss}(s_i^t) - (1 - \beta) \cdot \{ \max_{j < i, i \le |C^t|} sim(\mathbf{s}_i^t, \mathbf{s}_j^t) \}, \tag{14}$$

Here s_i^t denotes the i-th sentence in the candidate set when selecting the t-th sentence in snippet and β is a hyper-parameter ($\beta \in [0.1, 0.5]$). $sim(\cdot)$ is the cosine similarity of two vectors, and $\mathbf{s}_i^t$ is the distributed representation of s_i^t, which is generated by max-pooled GloVe [2] vectors of each word in s_i^t.

4   Experiments and Evaluation

In this section, we introduce the experimental setups as well as the results of the two evaluation methods: snippet quality evaluation and user preference test.

4.1   Data Collection and Processing

We extract search sessions from two real-world search logs recorded in 20170903 and 20180401 by *Sogou.com* (a major Chinese commercial search engine). The log data contains user ID, query word, search results, and click data. We adopt a standard 30 min. gap to split queries submitted by the same user into sessions. Sessions that are too short or too long (≤ 2 or ≥ 7 queries) are filtered because long sessions contain more noises but only account for little proportions while short sessions contain limited context information. We adopt jieba[2] for Chinese word segmentation. The webpage corpus is then fed into GloVe [2] to obtain word embeddings. Finally, the two log collections are organized into two datasets (SD_1 and SD_2) as shown in the first and second column of Table 1.

4.2   Snippet Quality Evaluation

We first use ROUGE [4] metrics to intrinsically measure the snippet quality. Then we collect reference snippets by user annotation and compare the generated snippets against the reference snippets for extrinsic evaluation.

---

[2] https://github.com/yanyiwu/cppjieba.

Annotation Process. We recruit 25 participants aged 19–24 to annotate the reference snippets. All of the participants are familiar with the basic operations of web search. Annotation data are randomly extracted from the two datasets (80 from SD_1 and 120 from SD_2). Basic statistics of this dataset (**SQE**) is presented in the third column of Table 1. Each participant needs to complete 40 tasks. In each task, the previous queries and result hyperlinks in the last query are presented to annotators. They need to read the result document and select the sentences that are most suitable for being included in the snippet with regard to user intent. The selected sentences should be pasted into an input box with a length limit of 110–165 Chinese characters (i.e., the average length of baseline snippets). All webpages receive five annotations and each of them will be regarded as a ground truth. On average, each participant spends 200 min to annotate 132 documents with a reward of about $8/h.

Baseline Methods. Few studies have focused on the context-aware summarization, so we take some typical summarization algorithms as baselines. We choose seven automatic summarizers implemented in the open-source tool SUMY[3], listed as *Luhn* [18], *Latent Semantic Analysis (LSA)* [19], *LexRank* [10], *TextRank* [11], *SumBasic* [20], *KL-Sum* [21] and *Reduction*. Another pseudo relevance feedback based method [7] is taken as the typical query-biased system for comparison (denoted by *PRF*). In addition, the snippets crawled from the *Sogou* search engine are also used as a baseline (denoted by *SE*). Note that although abstractive methods have developed a lot with the emergence of sophisticated deep learning models, they are not adaptive for commercial Web search engines, so we only consider the state-of-the-art extractive methods in this paper.

Table 2. Intrinsic evaluation results of each model. All values are $F_{1.2}$-scores, where ∗ and † indicate a statistically significant improvement over the strongest baseline *SE* at $p < 0.05/0.01$ level, respectively.

Sys.\Met.	RG-1	RG-2	RG-3	RG-4	RG-L	RG-W	RG-S	RG-SU
Luhn	0.236	0.167	0.148	0.136	0.215	0.101	0.119	0.122
KL-Sum	0.239	0.1663	0.147	0.136	0.215	0.101	0.118	0.122
Sumbasic	0.240	0.169	0.149	0.137	0.218	0.103	0.120	0.124
TextRank	0.242	0.171	0.151	0.139	0.220	0.103	0.122	0.125
PRF	0.361	0.209	0.151	0.111	0.309	0.120	0.155	0.161
SE(Sogou)	0.361	0.204	0.161	0.138	0.298	0.130	0.149	0.154
FMN_{NS}	0.352	0.216	0.185*	0.167†	0.283	0.131	0.157	0.161
FMN_{DS}	0.353	0.218	0.189*	0.172†	0.291	0.135	0.160	0.165
FMN_{SS}	**0.385** +6.48%	**0.259†** +26.54%	**0.226†** +40.15%	**0.205†** +48.34%	**0.314** +5.36%	**0.148*** +13.25%	**0.183†** +22.68%	**0.188†** +21.73%

⋆⋆ Note that RG is short for ROUGE. Here we only present the results of four systems with highest performances in SUMY: *Luhn, KL-Sum, SumBasic* and *TextRank*.

---

[3] https://github.com/miso-belica/sumy.

Overall Evaluation Results. We denote our approaches as FMN_{SS}, FMN_{NS} and FMN_{DS}, respectively. The results are presented in Table 2.

According to the results in Table 2, we have the following main findings:

- Generally, unsupervised summarization methods have the worst performance.
- By taking query content into consideration, *PRF* and *SE* achieve better performances than the query-independent baselines by a large margin.
- Systems that leverage the feedback memory mechanism to model search context achieve better performances in all metrics, especially in ROUGR-3/4. Such an improved performance on long phrase matching suggests a successful capture of users' session-level information needs.
- Among all models, FMN_{SS} that combines context-aware relevance score with TF-IDF term has the best overall performances. Especially, it achieves a 48.34% improvement over the *SE* baseline in ROUGE-4. Note that the models that utilize N-tuple Sorting (FMN_{NS}) and Diversified Sorting (FMN_{DS}) perform worse than FMN_{SS}. This indicates that forcing the algorithm to select consecutive sentences for the coherence and readability does not necessarily improve the snippet quality. Sentence-level consistency is enough for readers to get the main idea of the search result.

To sum up, the comparison results suggest that (1) the current query is crucial for search snippet generation; (2) the context information within a search session is helpful for snippet generation and that (3) our proposed method FMN_{SS} outperforms all the baseline systems.

Performances Across Session Lengths and Clicks. To investigate the impact of context information, we further analyze the model performances across sessions with different lengths and click numbers. Figure 2(a) shows the recall improvements of FMN_{SS} over *SE* in ROUGE-1 across different session lengths. We can observe that the improvement of FMN_{SS} over *SE* is generally larger when a session is longer (e.g., length = 5 or 6). Also from Fig. 2(b), we can find that our model can better exploit feedback information when there are more clicks in a session. Note that there is a drop in sessions with four queries, this may be caused by sparse click signals to be exploited by the feedback memory mechanism. Generally, our model can perform better by exploiting more clicks.

Ablation Study. To verify the results achieved by our model, we further compare the performance of each component in average ROUGE against the strongest baseline *SE* in Fig. 2(c). We delete the context information by feeding empty query history and clicks into the network and test the system performance. We can find that there is a huge drop in overall performance (+9.56% to −6.18% compared to *SE*) for FMN without context information. This reveals that context information is crucial for user modeling and snippet generation. Both the context information captured by FMN and the TF-IDF term contribute to system performance. The combination of all techniques has the highest improvement of 19.40% over *SE*, which indicates the effectiveness of our model.

(a) Impro. w.r.t. session len.   (b) Improv. w.r.t. clicks   (c) Ablation Study

Fig. 2. System performance in different conditions. Figure (a) and (b) show the performances improvement of FMN$_{SS}$ over SE in ROUGE-1 w.r.t. session lengths and click numbers. Figure (c) is the result of system ablation study.

4.3   User Preference Test

After evaluating the quality of the snippets generated by our models, we further explore whether people prefer the context-aware snippets by conducting a user preference test. To prepare data, we randomly extract 99 sessions from SD$_1$ and SD$_2$ to construct the annotation dataset. We then crawl the SERPs of the last queries in sessions from a search engine to expand the search results and generate snippets for them respectively. The annotation dataset is organized as **UPT**.

User perception on snippets is subtle, so it is both human- and time-consuming to conduct the side-by-side user preference test. We also pre-survey the user preferences among the baseline systems by collecting the annotation results in a small scope. The results have suggested that the SE system is much better than other baselines. So we only conduct a large-scale user preference test that compares the FMN$_{SS}$ (the best of our models) with the SE (the best baseline).

We recruit 45 participants aged from 17 to 25 to annotate their preferences for each pair of snippets. For each task, a search session and several pairs of snippets for the results of the last query in a session are presented to the participants. Similar to the snippet quality evaluation, the participants should take a glance at the query sequence and consider the search user's information needs. Then they need to click on the result page and skim the whole page from top to bottom. A pair of snippets for the page is presented vertically in the annotation page. The snippets share the same stylesheet as the original SERP but contain different contents generated by corresponding models. Modern web search engines may highlight some keywords in the snippet, which can influence the user's preference on the snippets. In this study, we only focus on the snippet content so we disable the keyword highlight feature. In addition, we also remove all the vertical results to avoid the influence of webpage layout and multimedia elements. Each participant should choose one snippet she prefers. The position of SE and testing snippets are randomly shuffled to avoid the position bias. In addition, to ensure the annotation quality, we impose a minimum annotation time by disabling the submit button for 15 s after the participant has entered the annotation page.

Table 3. The win/loss/tie cases for FMN$_{SS}$ compared to SE in different comparison conditions. Improvements of FMN$_{SS}$ over SE are calculated by $\frac{N_{win}-N_{loss}}{N_{win}+N_{loss}}$.

Conditions	Win	Loss	Tie	Improv.
All (100%)	448	410	26	+4.43%
Top 80%	384	311	24	+10.50%
Top 60%	290	229	19	**+11.75%**
Top 40%	191	156	12	+10.08%
Top 20%	95	79	8	+9.20%

Results and Analysis. Users' intents and information needs may shift within a search session. To this end, we calculate the cosine similarities between the max-pooled GloVe vectors of the last query and previous queries in each session and sort these sessions by the similarities in descending order. We then analyze the results of the preference test for five conditions, where top 20%, 40%, 60%, 80%, and all sessions are considered. The numbers of win/loss/tie cases of sessions across the five conditions are shown in Table 3. Figure 3(a) depicts the system improvements when filtering different proportions (from 0 to 60%) of sessions with an increasing similarity threshold. Although FMN$_{SS}$ model only has a 4.43% improvement over SE on all sessions, we find that once filtering some sessions with sharp intent shifts, the improvement will soon rise to over 10%. This can be explained by: feedbacks in previous search rounds can benefit those queries under the same topic to a greater extent. Intent shift may affect the system effectiveness thus should be considered in complex scenarios.

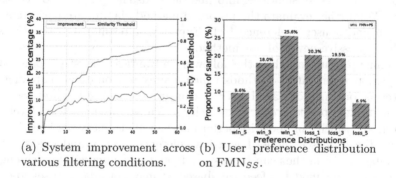

(a) System improvement across various filtering conditions.

(b) User preference distribution on FMN$_{SS}$.

Fig. 3. System performance w.r.t. filtering conditions and user preference distribution on FMN$_{SS}$. Note that on the right *win_n* represents $N_{win} - N_{loss} = n$ for FMN$_{SS}$ in a case and *loss_n* represents $N_{win} - N_{loss} = -n$.

The distribution of users' preferences over the FMN$_{SS}$ model and the baseline is shown in Fig. 3(b). We can observe that the distribution is skewed towards the "win" side, which indicates that the participants prefer the snippets generated by FMN$_{SS}$ over SE. Note that few cases have five consistent labels (e.g. the proportions of win_5 or $loss\_5$ are less than 10%), showing that user preference are diverse. To further ensure the robustness of evaluation results, we calculate average proportion scores and boolean scores of each case for SE and FMN$_{SS}$ in top 60% and all session conditions. The proportion score is the percentage of "win" within five labels. The boolean score is the majority vote of all preference judgments on a single pair. As shown in Table 4, all scores of the FMN$_{SS}$ model are higher than those of SE. The improvements in the proportion scores in both top 60% and all sessions condition are statistically significant. These results further demonstrate that users do prefer the snippets generated by the FMN$_{SS}$ model, especially in search scenarios without sharp intent shifts.

Table 4. The average proportion and boolean scores of SE and FMN$_{SS}$ in all and top 60% sessions conditions (* indicates a statistical significant improvement over SE with an independent t-test at $p < 0.01$, and σ^2 denotes the variance).

Score\Model	SE	FMN$_{SS}$	σ^2
Boolean (All)	0.4779	**0.5221**	0.2495
Percentage (All)	0.4804	**0.5196***	0.0825
Boolean (Top 60%)	0.4412	**0.5588***	0.2465
Percentage (Top 60%)	0.4683	**0.5317***	0.0800

5   Discussions and Conclusions

In this paper, we propose a novel model which adopts feedback memory mechanism to model users' session-level information needs and generate context-aware snippets. We further evaluate the proposed method via an automatic summary evaluation and a user preference test. Experiment results in both evaluation show the expressive power of our methods.

To sum up, our work has the following advantages. Firstly, compared to existing snippet generation methods which mainly rely on exact matching with query terms, our methods are better at capturing semantic features. Secondly, the model utilizes previous queries and clicks to model users' session-level information needs, which can boost its performance in multi-query sessions. Last but not least, the proposed model has a low inference latency and needs not any human labels to train thus can be easily adopted in commercial search engines. However, since our model is feedback-based, it may not adapt to sessions with dramatic intent shifts. Intent detection and search task identification methods should be explored for further improvement for context-aware snippets.

References

1. Wu, B., Xiong, C., Sun, M., et al.: Query suggestion with feedback memory network. In: Proceedings of the 2018 World Wide Web Conference, International World Wide Web Conferences Steering Committee, pp. 1563–1571 (2018)

2. Pennington, J., Socher, R., Manning, C.: Glove: Global vectors for word representation. In: Proceedings of the 2014 Conference on Empirical Methods in Natural Language Processing (EMNLP), pp. 1532–1543 (2014)
3. Maxwell, D., Azzopardi, L., Moshfeghi, Y.: A study of snippet length and informativeness: behaviour, performance and user experience. In: Proceedings of the 40th International ACM SIGIR Conference on Research and Development in Information Retrieval, pp. 35–144. ACM (2017)
4. Lin, C.Y.: Rouge: A package for automatic evaluation of summaries. In: Text Summarization Branches Out, pp. 74–81 (2004)
5. Wang, C., Jing, F., Zhang, L., et al.: Learning query-biased web page summarization. In: Proceedings of the Sixteenth ACM Conference on Information and Knowledge Management, pp. 555–562. ACM (2007)
6. Penin, T., Wang, H., Tran, T., Yu, Y.: Snippet generation for semantic web search engines. In: Domingue, J., Anutariya, C. (eds.) ASWC 2008. LNCS, vol. 5367, pp. 493–507. Springer, Heidelberg (2008). https://doi.org/10.1007/978-3-540-89704-0_34
7. Ko, Y., An, H., Seo, J.: An effective snippet generation method using the pseudo relevance feedback technique. In: Annual ACM Conference on Research and Development in Information Retrieval: Proceedings of the 30th Annual International ACM SIGIR Conference on Research and Development in Information Retrieval, pp. 711–712 (2007)
8. Sun, J.T., Shen, D., Zeng, H.J., et al.: Web-page summarization using clickthrough data. In: Proceedings of the 28th Annual International ACM SIGIR Conference on Research and Development in Information Retrieval, pp. 194–201. ACM (2005)
9. Chen, J., Mao, J., Liu, Y., Zhang, M., Ma, S.: Investigating query reformulation behavior of search users. In: Zhang, Q., Liao, X., Ren, Z. (eds.) CCIR 2019. LNCS, vol. 11772, pp. 39–51. Springer, Cham (2019). https://doi.org/10.1007/978-3-030-31624-2_4
10. Erkan, G., Radev, D.R.: Lexrank: Graph-based lexical centrality as salience in text summarization. J. Artif. Intell. Res. **22**, 457–479 (2004)
11. Mihalcea, R., Tarau, P.: Textrank: Bringing order into text. In: Proceedings of the 2004 Conference on Empirical Methods in Natural Language Processing, pp. 404–411 (2004)
12. Edmundson, H.P.: New methods in automatic extracting. J. ACM (JACM) **16**(2), 264–285 (1969)
13. Tombros, A., Sanderson, M., Gray, P.: Advantages of query biased summaries in information retrieval. In: SIGIR, pp. 2–10 (1998)
14. Chuklin, A., Markov, I., Rijke, M.: Click models for web search. Synth. Lect. Inf. Concepts Retrieval Serv. **7**(3), 1–115 (2015)
15. Chung, J., Gulcehre, C., Cho, K.H., et al.: Empirical evaluation of gated recurrent neural networks on sequence modeling (2014). arXiv:1412.3555
16. Carbonell, J.G., Goldstein, J.: The use of MMR, diversity-based reranking for reordering documents and producing summaries. In: SIGIR, pp. 335–336 (1998)
17. Kumar, V., Khattar, D., Gairola, S., et al.: Identifying clickbait: A multi-strategy approach using neural networks. In: The 41st International ACM SIGIR Conference on Research and Development in Information Retrieval, pp. 1225–1228. ACM (2018)
18. Luhn, H.P.: The automatic creation of literature abstracts. IBM J. Res. Dev. **2**(2), 159–165 (1958)
19. Steinberger, J., Jezek, K.: Using latent semantic analysis in text summarization and summary evaluation. Proc. ISIM **4**, 93–100 (2004)

20. Vanderwende, L., Suzuki, H., Brockett, C., et al.: Beyond SumBasic: Task-focused summarization with sentence simplification and lexical expansion. Inf. Process. Manage. **43**(6), 1606–1618 (2007)
21. Haghighi, A., Vanderwende, L.: Exploring content models for multi-document summarization. In: Proceedings of Human Language Technologies: The 2009 Annual Conference of the North American Chapter of the Association for Computational Linguistics, pp. 362–370. Association for Computational Linguistics (2009)
22. Ageev, M., Lagun, D., Agichtein, E.: Improving search result summaries by using searcher behavior data. In: Proceedings of the 36th International ACM SIGIR Conference on Research and Development in Information Retrieval, pp. 13–22. ACM (2013)

Investigating Fine-Grained Usefulness Perception Process in Mobile Search

Yukun Zheng, Jiaxin Mao, Yiqun Liu[✉], Xiaohui Xie, Min Zhang,
and Shaoping Ma

Department of Computer Science and Technology, Institute for Artificial Intelligence,
Beijing National Research Center for Information Science and Technology,
Tsinghua University, Beijing 100084, China
yiqunliu@tsinghua.edu.cn

Abstract. With the development and popularization of smartphones, search on mobile devices has become more and more popular in recent years. Existing research found that users' search interaction patterns in the mobile environment are different from those in the desktop environment. As we know, there are a number of vertical results and richly informative snippets in the ranked lists of mobile search engines. Users can perceive useful information from both the snippet and the landing page of a result. Therefore, we consider that it is necessary to investigate how users interact with mobile search engine result pages and their fine-grained usefulness perception processes. In this paper, we collected fine-grained usefulness annotations for mobile search results in a user study dataset. With the user behavior information in the dataset, we investigate the patterns of users' examination and click behavior and propose a user model for the fine-grained usefulness perception process in mobile search. Our research sheds light on improving user models in mobile search evaluation metrics and other mobile search-related applications.

Keywords: Mobile search · User behavior · Usefulness perception process

1 Introduction

Recently, more and more searches happen on mobile devices[1]. Mobile search is different from desktop search in both search context and user behavior patterns [3,10,13,14], and hence got widely studied recently. The differences between mobile and desktop search bring new challenges to search evaluation and other related tasks in mobile search. Meanwhile, results in both desktop and mobile search become more and more heterogeneous and have various presentation styles. Due to the smaller screen sizes, traffic cost and different interaction mechanisms of mobile search, mobile search engines tend to present results with rich information on SERPs to reduce the interaction cost of users. This causes that

---

[1] https://gs.statcounter.com/platform-market-share/desktop-mobile-tablet.

© Springer Nature Switzerland AG 2020
Z. Dou et al. (Eds.): CCIR 2020, LNCS 12285, pp. 17–28, 2020.
https://doi.org/10.1007/978-3-030-56725-5_2

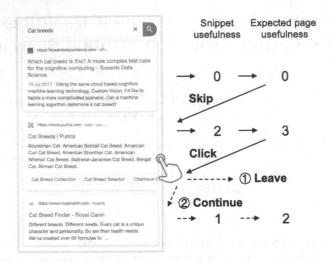

Fig. 1. A mobile SERP crawled from Google for the query "Cat breeds".

users may obtain demanded information from the result snippet without any click, which is called *click necessity bias* [18]. This phenomenon also appears in today's desktop search, e.g., the direct-answer results. However, the user models of most existing search evaluation metrics [1,2,9,12] don't take consideration of click necessity bias, which only take advantage of the relevance or the usefulness of results' landing pages, ignoring the snippet content of results. Thus, we consider that these traditional user models model users' information perception process in a rather coarse granularity.

Figure 1 shows a mobile SERP crawled from Google for the query "Cat breeds". Imagine that a user wants to know some names of common cat breeds and she starts examining the first result. Chances are she will skip this seemingly too professional and low useful result and then move her focus to the second one. The second result's snippet shows a number of cat breeds, seeming to be useful. Further, if she wants more information and expects the landing page of the second result to contain more cat breed names, she will probably click on the second result. After she reads the landing page of the second result, two possible future actions are: (1) If she finds enough useful information now, she may directly leave with high satisfaction; (2) Otherwise, she may continue examining the third result on the SERP. From this example of an imagined user, we find that users in mobile search perceive useful information in a finer-grained manner.

In this study, we first collect three fine-grained usefulness annotations for mobile search results in an existing user study dataset. Then, we make an analysis of the collected usefulness judgments to better understand how users perceive useful information during search processes. Next, we investigate how users examine and click on results as well as how they access and accumulate utility in mobile search based on the usefulness judgments. The main contributions are listed in three folds as follows:

- We firstly adopt the snippet usefulness, the expected page usefulness and the actual page usefulness in analyzing user behavior in mobile search.
- We make a thorough analysis on user behavior and propose a novel user model in the mobile search environment with the fine-grained usefulness perception process.
- We publicly release the annotations in this paper to support more information retrieval-related research.

2 Related Work

Compared to desktop search, mobile search performs in a smaller screen and usually displays less content on the screen. Different interaction mechanism leads to different user behavior patterns. Guo et al. [3] compared user interactions on web documents between the mobile and desktop scenarios. Raptis et al. [13] showed that how different screen sizes of mobile devices affect users' perceived usability, effectiveness and efficiency. As the first attempt to delve into examination behavior in mobile search, Lagun et al. [7] found that eye gaze behavior has a strong correlation with user satisfaction in mobile search. They further investigated searchers' attention on mobile SERPs with rich ad formats [8]. Kim et al. [5,6] conducted eye-tracking analysis of web search users on both large and small screens and found that users exhibited less eye movement, and were slower to complete tasks with smaller screens. Wang et al. [15] studied the users' examination behavior by examining the viewport logs of mobile search. Recently, Zheng et al. [19] examined fine-grained user examination behavior by taking viewports into consideration. They showed that users' attention varies with different stages of the search process.

The search behavior model of users can be used in evaluating search engines. A number of search evaluation approaches involve with hypothetical user browsing models. Moffat et al. [11] demonstrated that underlying user browsing models can be described by the continuation probability of search users while the continuation probability will be affected by different aspects. The continuation probability at the i-th position means the probability that the user examine the next document after she examined the i-th document (i.e., $P(E_{i+1} = 1|E_i = 1)$). For example, Järvelin and Kekäläinen [4] proposed a metric, DCG, that discounts the weight assigned to documents further down the ranking. RBP [12] assumes that users examine the $(i + 1)$-th result after examining the i-th result with persistence ρ and will end their examination with probability $1 - \rho$. Besides considering the position impact, ERR [2] takes result relevance (user gain) into consideration. And Zhang et al. [17] tried to model the search process based on upper limits for both benefits and costs, and proposed a Bejeweled Player Model (BPM). Recently, Luo et al. [9] linked the discount process with the height of each examined snippet and landing page, and proposed Height Biased Gain (HBG) for mobile search.

However, the user models of existing evaluation metrics we discussed above don't take the finer-grained usefulness perception process into consideration. Our contributions in this paper complement existing work by investigating how different variants of usefulness affect users' search behavior, especially for examination behavior and click behavior. Our findings shed light on the design of evaluation metrics for mobile search.

3   Data Collection

3.1   Overview of THUIR-Mobile Dataset

We first introduce the dataset used in this paper, which is a user study dataset named Tiangong-Mobile created by [19][2]. This dataset was constructed on the basis of a mobile search-related user study. In each search task of this user study, a query and a description of the corresponding search background was presented. The participant freely browsed a given mobile SERP to look for useful information and complete the search task. This dataset consists of task data, user behavior data, multiple crowdsourcing annotations and etc.

Table 1. The statistics of the dataset from Tiangong-Mobile.

#Users	#Tasks	#Valid sessions	#Unique results	#Unique clicks
13	55	439	550	727

Task. We check all 60 tasks and discard five tasks where some of the first 10 results are missed in the dataset. In the remained 55 tasks, there are 10 navigational, 24 informational and 21 transactional queries. The SERPs in Tiangong-Mobile dataset are crawled from Sogou, a commercial search engine in China. On each SERP, there are about 22 results of which top 3 results are examined by users at most cases. In that regard, we only keep the first 10 results on each SERP in the later usefulness annotation. Tiangong-Mobile provides position information of search results on the SERPs, based on which we can use to match the results with the eye-gazing data. Table 1 shows statistics of the dataset used in this study.

User Behavior. Various user behavior data on the mobile device during search tasks is available in Tiangong-Mobile, including scrolling, clicks and the eye-tracking data. There are 727 unique clicks in total, as shown in Table 1. Specifically, the eye-tracker records two kinds of eye-tracking data, i.e., fixation and saccade. Existing eye-tracking studies treat fixation (i.e., eye-gazing behavior) as the measure of user attention, we follow the sa!tme principle in the later analysis in Sect. 4.1.

---

[2] http://www.thuir.cn/data-wsdm20-UserStudy/.

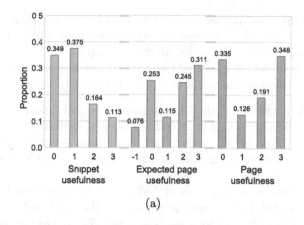

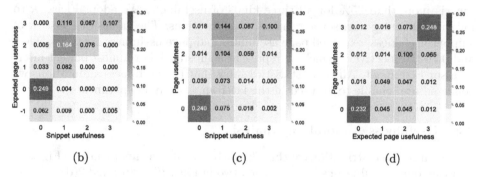

Fig. 2. (a) the distributions of three kinds of usefulness, (b) the joint distribution of U^s and EU^p, (c) the joint distribution of U^s and U^p, and (d) the joint distribution of EU^p and U^p.

Crowdsourcing Annotations. Tiangong-Mobile provides multiple crowdsourcing annotations, such as click necessity and result type. There are various heterogeneous results in this mobile search dataset. According to the result type labels, there are 18 result types for both organic and vertical results. Vertical results can be further categorized into many specific types, such as direct answer, knowledge, encyclopedia, video and etc.

3.2 Collecting Usefulness Annotations

We recruit three distinct groups of well-trained workers to annotate three kinds of usefulness for each search result respectively according to the corresponding snippet screenshot and content of landing pages:

- **Snippet usefulness**, which is labeled only based on the visible content of the result snippet to measure how useful the snippet content is to satisfy the information need.

- **Expected page usefulness**, which is labeled based on the snippet content to measure how useful the corresponding landing page will be to satisfy the information need after the user examines the snippet.
- **Page usefulness**, which is labeled based on the content of the result's landing page to measure how useful the landing page is to satisfy the information need.

We adopt a four-grade criteria (0: usefulness; 1: slightly useful; 2: moderately useful; 3: highly useful) to annotate the three kinds of usefulness as same as that in Wu et al. [16]. There are 42 unclickable results such as direct answer results, i.e., they have no corresponding landing pages. For these results, we label their expected page usefulness as -1.

In the annotation study, we collect judgments for each search result from three different annotators and use the median as the final usefulness label. To ensure the reliability of annotations, we conduct quality inspection and the accuracy is more than 95% for all three kinds of usefulness. We adopt Fleiss' κ to measure the inter-assessor agreement of annotations. The values of Fleiss' κ of snippet usefulness, expected page usefulness and page usefulness are 0.754, 0.810 and 0.762, respectively, which all represent a substantial or almost perfect inter-assessor agreement. All these statistics show that the usefulness annotations we collected are reliable to be used in the later analysis and experiments[3].

3.3   Usefulness Annotation Analysis

We examine the distributions of three kinds of usefulness annotations in Fig. 2(a) and the joint distributions between each two in Figs. 2(b), 2(c) and 2(d). We use U^s, EU^p and U^p to denote snippet usefulness, expected page usefulness and page usefulness in this paper.

Snippet Usefulness. Figure 2(a) shows that more than 70% of snippets are useless or slightly useful, which is because snippets are usually short and contain little information. Only 11.3% of snippets can completely satisfy users' information needs such as direct answer results.

Expected Page Usefulness. Only 36.8% of results' landing pages are expected as useless or slightly useful, while more than 55% of results have a moderate or high expected page usefulness. Figure 2(b) shows that in 40.5% of cases, the expected page usefulness of a result is higher than its snippet usefulness, while the two usefulness are equal to each other in 51.4% of cases. Only 2 results in our dataset have higher snippet usefulness than their expected page usefulness. We examine these two results and find that they are from web sites with little credibility and reliability. The aforementioned findings show that in most cases, users estimate the landing page not less useful than its corresponding snippet. We consider that the different expectations for the landing page of users may lead to different search behavior which will be discussed in Sect. 4.1.

---

[3] We will publicly release the collected usefulness judgments after the review.

Page Usefulness. Highly useful results account for 34.8%, while useless results are also up to 33.5%. We compare page usefulness with snippet usefulness in Fig. 2(c). There are 12.3% of cases where page usefulness is lower than snippet usefulness, which is mostly caused by the bad quality of the landing pages. When useless content occupies the major area of the landing page, it's extremely difficult for people to find useful information in it, so they will give a rather low page usefulness, even lower than its snippet usefulness. There are also 40.6% of cases where page usefulness is higher than snippet usefulness, indicating that users can get more benefits from clicking on these kinds of results and browsing landing pages. In Fig. 2(d), we compare expected page usefulness with snippet usefulness. We can find that in 62.9% of cases, the user can expect accurate page usefulness based on the result snippet, i.e., the expected page usefulness is equal to the actual page usefulness. However, there are 22.6% of cases where the user has a higher expectation for the usefulness of a landing page than its actual page usefulness. In addition, there also exist 14.5% of cases where the user underestimates how useful a landing page will be after only examining its snippet.

4   Usefulness-Perceived Gain

In this section, we first investigate patterns of users' examination behavior and click behavior in mobile search with aforementioned three kinds of usefulness. Next, we construct a user model with a finer-grained usefulness perception process. We aim to answer following research questions:

- **RQ1:** What's the relationship between the accumulated utility and the continuation probability?
- **RQ2:** What's the impact of snippet and expected page usefulness on user attention?
- **RQ3:** How does snippet and expected page usefulness affect users click behavior at different ranking positions?

4.1   User Behavior Analysis

Examination Behavior. First, we examine how the accumulated utility during the search process affects users' examination behavior. In our dataset, before a user stops browsing, she will examine three results per session on average, including one highly useful result, which shows that highly useful results can mostly satisfy users' information needs in sessions of our dataset and this meets our usefulness criteria. There are many possible estimation approaches for the accumulated utility of users. For instance, we only use the maximum utility among all examined results as the accumulated utility in this work. The utility g_i of the i-th result in a search session is calculated based on its usefulness as:

$$g_i = I(C_i = 0) * g_i^s + I(C_i = 1) * \max(g_i^s, g_i^p) \tag{1}$$

$$g_i^s = 2^{U_i^s} - 1, \ U_i^s \in \{0, 1, 2, 3\} \tag{2}$$

$$g_i^p = 2^{U_i^p} - 1, \ U_i^p \in \{0, 1, 2, 3\} \tag{3}$$

Table 2. Continuation probabilities given the maximum utility of examined results.

Maximum utility	0	1	3	7
Continuation prob.	1.000	0.970	0.904	0.751
#Cases	447	165	354	1403

Table 3. The average reading time and height-normalized reading time of examined results given snippet usefulness (U^s) and expected page usefulness (EU^p). The units of reading time and a result's height are one millisecond and one pixel on the screen, respectively.

Reading time		U^s			
		0	1	2	3
EU^p	−1	820.5/1.220	1029.9/2.217	-	1957.5/3.048
	0	812.7/2.130	834.0/0.979	-	-
	1	1036.7/2.274	982.4/2.103	-	-
	2	1259.2/2.479	1302.0/2.519	1292.7/2.634	-
	3	-	2128.3/3.401	2075.1/3.140	2202.7/2.995

where g_i^s and g_i^p denote the utility of the result's snippet and landing page, respectively, while $I(C_i = 1)$ and $I(C_i = 0)$ denote that the user clicked or didn't click on this result in the session. Formally, the accumulated utility AU_i after examining the i-th result is given as $\max(AU_{i-1}, g_i)$ under the maximum utility assumption. Specially, we set AU_0 to 0, denoting that the user access no accumulated utility before examining the SERP.

With the viewport logs, we can obtain the results which have been exposed on the screen. With the viewport logs, we select the clicked results and results whose reading time (i.e., eye-gazing duration) is no less than 200 ms [19] from all exposed results. Then, we treated the result with the lowest rank in the selected results as the last examined result, and hence we can calculate the probability of continuing examining. Table 2 shows the continuation probability given the accumulated utility estimated by the maximum examined utility. We observe a significant decay of the continuation probability as the accumulated utility increases.

We are here to address **RQ1**. According to our findings in the Tiangong-Mobile dataset, the larger the accumulated gain is (i.e., a larger degree of the user's information need is satisfied), the more likely she is to stop examining the ranked list.

Next, we investigate how snippet usefulness and expected page usefulness affect users' eye-tracking behavior on SERPs to address **RQ2**. Table 3 shows the user attention on results given snippet usefulness and expected page usefulness. We find that no matter how useful the snippet is, the results with the same

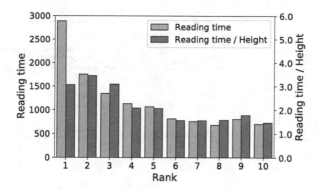

Fig. 3. The average reading time and height-normalized reading time of examined results given the result rank. The units of reading time and a result's height are one millisecond and one pixel on the screen, respectively.

Table 4. Click probabilities given the snippet usefulness (U^s), expected page usefulness (EU^p) and result rank.

$P(C|U^s, EU^p, Rank)$		(U^s, EU^p)					
		(3, 3)	(2, 3)	(1, 3)	(2, 2)	(1, 2)	Others
Rank	[1, 2]	0.796	0.895	0.844	0.550	0.595	0.139
	[3, 4]	0.846	0.735	0.641	1.000	0.556	0.306
	≥5	0.867	0.500	0.556	0.400	0.577	0.274
	[1, 10]	0.806	0.786	0.757	0.529	0.580	0.251

expected page usefulness attract similar user attention. The higher expected page usefulness a result has, the more attention it receives from users. In a word, the expected page usefulness dominates more in the users' attention than snippet usefulness. Figure 3 shows the average reading time on results at different ranks and the average reading time normalized by result heights. Considering these two variants of reading time as the measures of user attention on a result, we observe an obvious decay of user attention as the rank increases from 1 to 6, while user attention becomes stable after rank 6.

Click Behavior. With click data in Tiangong-Mobile and the collected usefulness annotations, we are able to investigate how the snippet usefulness and expected page usefulness impact users' clicks. Table 4 shows the statistics of click probabilities given the snippet usefulness, expected page usefulness and result rank. Due to the sparsity issue with clicks, we categorize ten result ranks into three intervals: [1, 2], [3, 4] and [5, 10]. Then we divide all examined results into several groups with different snippet usefulness, expected page usefulness and rank intervals. We calculate the probability for each group by averaging #Click/#Examination over all the results in the group.

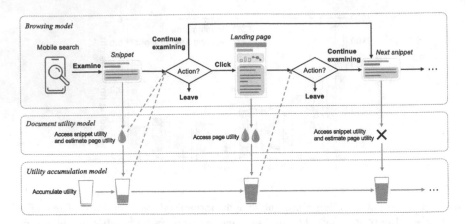

Fig. 4. An illustration of the hypothetical user model in mobile search.

Now we can address our **RQ3** here based on Table 4. When (U^s, EU^p) is $(3,3)$, the click probability of these results keeps at a relatively high level at all ranks and has a slight increase with the rank. However, for results with $(2,3)$ or $(1,3)$, their click probabilities degrade dramatically when the rank increases. This indicates that higher snippet usefulness can help results at low ranks attract more clicks. For $(3, 3)$, $(2,3)$ and $(1,3)$ at rank $[1,2]$, we find that the click probability of $(2, 3)$ is the highest, followed by $(1, 3)$, while $(3, 3)$ has the lowest click probability. We think the reason behind is that users tend to click the results whose snippet shows the evidence to provide useful information at high ranking positions. So that the corresponding landing page is expected to contain more benefits. For results with $(1, 2)$, we can see that their click probabilities are rather stable in different rank intervals. When we compare results at all ten ranks, we can find that higher snippet usefulness and higher expected page usefulness of a result usually lead to a higher click probability.

4.2   User Model for Mobile Search

Based on the observations of our dataset, we distill a new user model for mobile search. Figure 4 illustrates the user model that we propose for mobile search. Since we consider that the utility of a document only depends on its usefulness with respect to the query, we don't distinguish between usefulness and utility here. The C/W/L framework [11] is a general user model for evaluating search engines, including three sub-models: browsing model, document utility model and utility accumulation model. Our user model follows the C/W/L framework. Zheng et al. [19] studied Tiangong-Mobile dataset and found that users generally follow a top-down order to examine SERPs in mobile search scenarios. Therefore, we adopt the linear browsing order in our user model, which assumes the user examines the ranked list sequentially from top to bottom until she stops at a certain position. After examining a result's snippet, the user accesses snippet utility and accumulates the utility, while she also estimates the utility for the page at the same time. Next, she will decide whether to click on this result or not. If the user doesn't click, she will judge whether the current accumulated utility is enough for leaving, and if not enough, she needs to continue examining the next result's snippet on the SERP. Otherwise, if she clicks on the result, she will access utility from the landing page and also accumulates utility. After browsing the landing page, she needs to decide whether to leave or not according to the current accumulated utility. And if she doesn't leave, this process will continue repeating until she leaves. During the search process, the attention of the user gradually degrades. Meanwhile, the user's clicks are also biased by the snippet utility, expected page utility and result rank. We assume the user accesses the whole utility of the snippet and landing page once she examines them. Compared to user models in existing search evaluation metrics, this proposed user model takes the finer-grained utility (or usefulness) perception process into account.

5   Conclusion and Future Work

In this paper, we have investigated fine-grained usefulness in mobile search scenarios. We have collected three variants of usefulness for search results, i.e., snippet usefulness, expected page usefulness and page usefulness in an existing user study dataset on mobile search. Equipped with the usefulness data and user behavior data, we have thoroughly studied how variants of usefulness affect user behavior, i.e., the continuation probability, user attention and user clicks, and obtain several insightful findings: (1) The continuation probability decreases when the maximum utility of all examined result increases; (2) The expected page usefulness has a stronger influence on user attention than the snippet usefulness; (3) Higher snippet usefulness and higher expected page usefulness of a search result usually lead to a higher click probability. On the basis of observations gained from the data analysis, we have proposed a new user model for mobile search.

Limitations of the proposed user model which may guide future work include the following: (1) The continuation probability may be affected by other factors and the accumulated utility can also be calculated in other ways. We leave this as one of the future works. (2) In the user model, we only investigate the effect of fine-grained usefulness on user attention and ignore a lot of other known factors, such as result type and presentation styles. In the future, we should take these factors into consideration and make a more comprehensive analysis.

Acknowledgements. This work is supported by the National Key Research and Development Program of China (2018YFC0831700) and Natural Science Foundation of China (Grant No. 61622208, 61732008, 61532011).

References

1. Bailey, P., Moffat, A., Scholer, F., Thomas, P.: User variability and IR system evaluation. In: SIGIR 2015, pp. 625–634. ACM (2015)
2. Chapelle, O., Metlzer, D., Zhang, Y., Grinspan, P.: Expected reciprocal rank for graded relevance. In: CIKM 2009, pp. 621–630. ACM (2009)
3. Guo, Q., Jin, H., Lagun, D., Yuan, S., Agichtein, E.: Mining touch interaction data on mobile devices to predict web search result relevance. In: SIGIR 2013, pp. 153–162. ACM (2013)
4. Järvelin, K., Kekäläinen, J.: IR evaluation methods for retrieving highly relevant documents. In: SIGIR 2000, pp. 41–48. ACM (2000)
5. Kim, J., Thomas, P., Sankaranarayana, R., Gedeon, T., Yoon, H.J.: Eye-tracking analysis of user behavior and performance in web search on large and small screens. J. Assoc. Inf. Sci. Technol. **66**(3), 526–544 (2015)
6. Kim, J., Thomas, P., Sankaranarayana, R., Gedon, T., Yoon, H.J.: Understanding eye movements on mobile devices for better presentation designs of search results. J. Am. Soc. Inf. Sci. Technol. (2015)
7. Lagun, D., Hsieh, C.H., Webster, D., Navalpakkam, V.: Towards better measurement of attention and satisfaction in mobile search. In: SIGIR 2014, pp. 113–122. ACM (2014)
8. Lagun, D., McMahon, D., Navalpakkam, V.: Understanding mobile searcher attention with rich ad formats. In: CIKM 2016, pp. 599–608. ACM (2016)
9. Luo, C., Liu, Y., Sakai, T., Zhang, F., Zhang, M., Ma, S.: Evaluating mobile search with height-biased gain. In: SIGIR 2017, pp. 435–444. ACM (2017)
10. Mao, J., Luo, C., Zhang, M., Ma, S.: Constructing click models for mobile search. In: SIGIR 2018, p. 775–784. ACM (2018)
11. Moffat, A., Thomas, P., Scholer, F.: Users versus models: What observation tells us about effectiveness metrics. In: CIKM 2013, pp. 659–668. ACM (2013)
12. Moffat, A., Zobel, J.: Rank-biased precision for measurement of retrieval effectiveness. ACM Trans. Inf. Syst. **27**(1), 1–27 (2008)
13. Raptis, D., Tselios, N., Kjeldskov, J., Skov, M.B.: Does size matter?: Investigating the impact of mobile phone screen size on users' perceived usability, effectiveness and efficiency. In: MobileHCI 2013, pp. 127–136. ACM (2013)
14. Song, Y., Ma, H., Wang, H., Wang, K.: Exploring and exploiting user search behavior on mobile and tablet devices to improve search relevance. In: WWW 2013, pp. 1201–1212. ACM (2013)
15. Wang, X., Su, N., He, Z., Liu, Y., Ma, S.: A large-scale study of mobile search examination behavior. In: SIGIR 2018, pp. 1129–1132. ACM (2018)
16. Wu, Z., Mao, J., Liu, Y., Zhang, M., Ma, S.: Investigating passage-level relevance and its role in document-level relevance judgment. In: SIGIR 2019, pp. 605–614. ACM (2019)
17. Zhang, F., Liu, Y., Li, X., Zhang, M., Xu, Y., Ma, S.: Evaluating web search with a bejeweled player model. In: SIGIR 2017, pp. 425–434. ACM (2017)
18. Zheng, Y., Mao, J., Liu, Y., Luo, C., Zhang, M., Ma, S.: Constructing click model for mobile search with viewport time. ACM Trans. Inf. Syst. **37**(4), 1–34 (2019)
19. Zheng, Y., Mao, J., Liu, Y., Sanderson, M., Zhang, M., Ma, S.: Investigating examination behavior in mobile search. In: WSDM 2020. ACM (2020)

ResFusion: A Residual Learning Based Fusion Framework for CTR Prediction

Junmei Bao[1], Yangguang Ji[1], Yonghui Yang[1], Le Wu[1,2(✉)], and Ruiji Fu[2]

[1] School of Computer Science and Information Engineering,
Hefei University of Technology, Hefei 230009, China
hfut.baojunmei@gmail.com, jyguang1997@gmail.com, yyh.hfut@gmail.com,
lewu.ustc@gmail.com
[2] State Key Laboratory of Cognitive Intelligence,
iFLYTEK, Hefei, People's Republic of China
rjfu@iflytek.com

Abstract. CTR prediction tasks deal with the problem of evaluating the probability of users clicking on products, and have been widely deployed in many online recommendation and advertising platforms. Mainstream CTR models can be divided into two categories: the traditional machine learning models (e.g., GBDT [7]) that learn the linear feature combinations for prediction, and deep learning based algorithms (such as DeepFM [9]) for modeling the complex and sparse feature correlations. Some recent works proposed to fuse these two kinds of models for prediction. These fusion models either feed the intermediate results learned by one model into the second category or rely on the ensemble techniques to fuse two independently trained model outputs. In this paper, we propose a residual learning based fusion framework for CTR prediction. The key idea is that, we first train a model (e.g., GBDT), and let the second model (e.g., DeepFM) learn the residual part that can not be accurately predicted by the first model. The soundness of this framework is that: as the prediction power of these two kinds of models is complementary, it is easier to let the second model learn the residual output that can not be well captured by the first model. We show that our proposed framework is flexible and it is easier to train with faster convergence. Extensive experimental results on three real-world datasets show the effectiveness of our proposed framework.

Keywords: CTR prediction · Gradient Boosting Decision Tree (GBDT) · Deep Neural Network (DNN) · Models fusion

1 Introduction

With the prevalence of intelligent mobile devices, a huge volume of online transactions and browsing data has become available. Given huge number of items, Click Rate Prediction (CTR) has become a dominant element on these platforms. Specifically, CTR prediction focuses on predicting the likelihood of a user

© Springer Nature Switzerland AG 2020
Z. Dou et al. (Eds.): CCIR 2020, LNCS 12285, pp. 29–41, 2020.
https://doi.org/10.1007/978-3-030-56725-5_3

clicking an item, and the predicted items with larger probability can be displayed for users.

As CTR prediction is usually deemed as a classification problem in CTR prediction [4,8,9,11,14,16], current solutions could be divided into two categories: traditional machine learning based models [3,6,21] and deep learning based models [5,9,13,17,22]. As one of the proved most effective models among traditional machine learning based approaches, GBDT [7] constructs a tree structure by iteratively selecting the feature with the most significant statistical information gain, which is more conducive to automatically combining some dense numerical features, but it is impossible to learn very well for high-dimensional sparse category features [16]. Recently, DeepFM [9], as a representative deep learning based models, models the complex and hidden correlations between features for prediction, nevertheless, it's learning performance for dense digital features is not good enough. In fact, these two kinds of models are complementary, and jointly considering them would facilitate learning both the linear and non-linear features, in order to further enhance performance of either model.

The current solutions for combining the different models can be mainly classified into two categories: [1,11,18,24,25]: either to feed the intermediate results learned by one model into the second category [11,18,24,25], or to rely on the ensemble techniques to fuse two independently trained model outputs [1,18]. These models show the advantages of modeling both the linear and non-linear features together, and lead to better performance in practice. However, we argue that: since different models capture different characteristics of the data, instead of fusing them simply, could we design a better fusion model that more explicitly utilizes the different prediction power of these two kinds of models? Considering the above characteristics, exploring how to use the respective advantages of GBDT and NN, and merging the two types of models effectively to solve the one-sided problem in feature learning seem critical.

In this paper, we propose a fusion framework learning strategy, based on the idea of ResNet [10], to improve the CTR prediction in real world data. The key idea is that, we first train a model (e.g., GBDT), and let the second model (e.g., DeepFM) learn the residual part that can not be accurately predicted by the first model. In fact, our proposed framework is an extension of the residual learning in the deep architecture design into model fusion for CTR prediction. Then, we analyze the soundness of this framework: as the prediction power of these two kinds of models is complementary, it is easier to let the second model learn the residual output that can not be well captured by the first model. We also show that our proposed framework is flexible and it is easier to train with faster convergence. Finally, extensive experimental results on three real-world datasets clearly show the effectiveness of our proposed model for the CTR prediction tasks.

2   Problem Definition and Related Works

2.1   Problem Definition

In a CTR prediction system, usually we can obtain the users' historical click records $D = \{(x_i, y_i)\}$ about the products. Let $x_i \in \mathbb{R}^d$ denote each sample with d features including numerical features and categorical features, and $y_i = \{0, 1\}$ denote observed label representing whether user clicks item. The CTR prediction task can be formulated as a supervised classification problem as follows:

Definition 1 (Click-Through Rate Prediction). *Given the training datasets $D_{train} = \{(x_{train}, y_{train})\}$, our goal is to learn a mapping function $f(x)$ that satisfies $\hat{y}_{train} = f(x_{train})$ reaching as much closer to y_{train} as possible. Then, for test datasets $D_{test} = \{x_{test}\}$, we compute $\hat{y}_{test} = f(x_{test})$ for user x_{test} to denote whether users will click on items.*

2.2   Related Works

In this section, we will mainly introduce the related works of the current CTR prediction tasks from the following three aspects: Traditional Machine Learning Models, Deep Neural Network Models and current Fusion Models.

Traditional Machine Learning Models. Logistic Regression is a generalized CTR prediction model that linearly combines each feature, it has been widely used in large-scale classification tasks due to its simplicity and low time complexity [20]. Apart from the linear combination of individual features, Factorization Machine (FM) [19] enumerates extra second-order cross information of all features and sends them into the model on the basis of LR. Field-aware Factorization Machines (FFM) [13] introduces the concept of field and assumes that each feature has different feature embeddings respectively for the different cross fields. Some other prevalent CTR prediction models derive from ensemble approaches. These approaches lie in three aspects: 1). **Boosting** works for the under-fitting models with high bias and low variance. For instance, AdaBoost [6] algorithm is one earliest classical implementation of the boosting algorithms, which is essentially a strong classifier constructed by a linear combination of multiple weak classifiers. Subsequently, some more effective gradient boosting methods, like GBDT [7], have been proposed as the promotion of AdaBoost algorithm by optimizing the loss function based on a negative gradient descent method. 2). **Bagging** approaches work for the instance of data with high variance but low bias. And Bagging could alleviate the high variance problems by bootstrap sampling from data. 3). **Stacking** could instead work for both variance and bias problems. It introduces a meta learner for aggregating heterogeneous component strong classifiers, which distinguishes the most from the former two approaches.

Deep Neural Network Models. Recently, many deep learning based CTR models have been proposed [5,9,17]. These models, focusing on how to more effectively model non-linear feature interactions, have been successfully applied to many industrial scenarios. Among them, Wide & Deep [5] can jointly learn by both the wide linear models and deep neural networks, which captures the low-order and high-order cross features. Besides, DeepFM [9] exceeds FM in extracting high-order combined features learnt by additional DNN parts, which can automatically combine high-order features without manual intervention in an end-to-end manner. Last but not least, xDeepFM [17] introduces a significant structure of the compressed interactive network (CIN) to generate feature interactions in an explicit fashion. Graph Convolutional Networks (GCNs) [2,23] iteratively encode graph structure and node features for node representation, which could capture the hidden feature interactions for CTR prediction.

Fusion Models. Since GBDT and NN models are suitable respectively for numerical features and categorical features, a growing number of methods emerge about how to fuse these two kinds of models for higher accuracy in prediction. These fusion models can be divided into the following two categories:

1) **Feature Fusion.** This kind of fusion models utilize the first model's results as additional features to train the second model. There are some fusion works directly combining the GBDT with NN on the feature level. In other words, they use one model's learning output results as additional feature inputs to feed into a second model with the same original data. For instance, we can extract leaf nodes of a pre-trained GBDT as a series of features input and then put them into a new model. Many works [11,18,25] have proved the effectiveness of this method, such as GBDT+LR [11] model which uses leaf nodes information trained by GBDT as combined features for LR training and GBDT2DNN [18] is a cascading fusion model that first trains a GBDT model, and the predicting score of GBDT is fed as an input feature into the DNN model. So this kind of fusion methods can be understood as a cascade process of feature engineering plus model learning.

2) **Prediction Fusion.** Another kind of fusion models usually intuitively combine the two model predictions by learning ensemble weights. In this way, $\overline{DNN + GBDT}$ [18] proposes to take a weighted average of prediction scores learnt separately from DNN and GBDT models sharing common training data and outputs the final probability score after an activation function. Another model named MTRecS-DLT [1] directly fuses the output scores of two single models in the ratio of 1:1 without using the *sigmoid* function.

In summary, traditional machine learning based models can accomplish linear feature combinations, and NN models use embedding strategy to solve complex feature intersections. Nevertheless, when they are faced with large-scale, heterogeneous data, one single model is no more effective because of their respective weaknesses. In addition, the existing fusion methods also have some notable shortcomings. For feature fusion models, only a single model is used as a feature extraction process, failing to directly combine the complementary advantages of the two types of models. Besides, in terms of prediction fusion models, an additional ensemble frame is needed to fuse the results of two single models. The quality of the final prediction results depends excessively on the fusion ability of the additional ensemble frame. Therefore, based on the above characteristics, we propose a residual learning based fusion framework to alleviate the limitation of existing fusion methods. Figure 1 shows the differences between the existing fusion models and the ResFusion framework which we proposed.

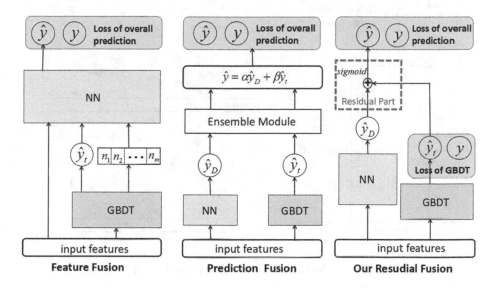

Fig. 1. The differences between our model and other fusion model

3   The Proposed Framework

In this section, we would introduce our proposed ResFusion framework for CTR prediction tasks in detail. We begin with the integral architecture, followed by the details of model components. At the end of this section, we would demonstrate the model training process and the discussion of our ResFusion framework.

3.1   Overall ResFusion Framework Architecture

The Fig. 2 shows the integral architecture of the ResFusion. By taking a feature set $X(x_1, x_2, x_3......x_d)$ as input, it outputs the probability $\hat{y}$ that user would like to click the item (e.g., web pages or ads). The overall architecture of our model contains two main parts: the GBDT component and the DeepFM component. Specifically, by taking the related inputs, the GBDT outputs probability $\hat{y}_t$.

Then we can calculate the residual between the true label y and the predicted value of GBDT $\hat{y}_t$, and we called this value as res_t, which is the key of our model. Next, the residuals are sent into the DeepFM component as the new learning target, with the same input features as GBDT's. Then the DeepFM part would output residual prediction value $\hat{y}_D$, for complementary of GBDT component. The model will finally get the predicted value, which can be expressed as: $\hat{y} = \hat{y}_D + \hat{y}_t$. We detail each part used in our fusion model as follows:

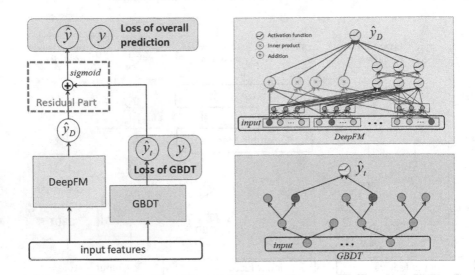

Fig. 2. The overall architecture of ResFusion

GBDT. GBDT is a decision tree algorithm based on the gradient boosting framework and can be seen on the right of the Fig. 2. "Gradient boost" means that each iteration process is to reduce the residual of the previous iteration, and a new weak classifier model is established in the direction of the gradient of the residual reduction. So the essence of GBDT algorithm can be expressed as the boosting method based decision tree:

$$F_M(x) = \sum_{m=1}^{M} T(x, \gamma_m) \tag{1}$$

Where $T(x, \gamma_m)$ represents the decision tree, γ_m represents the parameter of the tree, and M is the number of trees. And strong classifier $F_M(x)$ can be composed of multiple weak classifiers $T(x, \gamma_m)$ linear added. And by training a GBDT, we can get the prediction score $\hat{y}_t$.

Then we can compute the residual as:

$$res_t = y - \hat{y}_t \tag{2}$$

DeepFM. DeepFM is a neural network-based factorization machine (FM). Moreover, the model structure can be found in the right of the Fig. 2. This method contains two inner parts: FM part and DNN part. The FM part learns mainly from primary and second-order cross features as low-order features, while the deep part is a feed-forward neural network to extracts high-order cross features. FM and DNN share the standard features' input by linking with the common input layers and embedding layers. Finally, we combine the results of DNN y_{DNN} and FM y_{FM} and send them into an activate function. The final prediction result of DeepFM component is summed as:

$$\hat{y}_D(x_n) = y_{DNN}(x_n) + y_{FM}(x_n) \tag{3}$$

Then we sum the output of two components: $\hat{y}_t$, $\hat{y}_D$, and obtain the final prediction score $\hat{y} = \hat{y}_t + \hat{y}_D$.

3.2 Model Training

As our model contains two components, we first train a strong classifier called GBDT through the process of fitting the residuals by multiple iterations. The loss function for optimizing the tree model in every iteration process is:

$$\gamma_m = \arg\min_{\gamma} \sum_{n=1}^{N} \mathcal{L}(y_n, F_{m-1}(x_n) + T(x_n, \gamma)) \tag{4}$$

and the prediction score of GBDT $\hat{y}_t$ is used to calculate the residual with the true label y, and then the DeepFM try to fit this residual by optimizing the following formula:

$$W = \arg\min_{W} \sum_{n=1}^{N} \mathcal{L}(y_n, s(\hat{y}_D(x_n) + \hat{y}_t(x_n))) \tag{5}$$

where $s(x)$ is a *sigmoid* function, above two loss we all use *logloss* function to complete a binary classification task. γ and W represent the model parameters of GBDT and DeepFM. In practice, we use the *LightGBM* [15] to train a GBDT model, then we implement the DeepFM model with Pytorch[1] to train model parameters with mini-batch Adam.

3.3 Discussions

In this section, We would discuss our proposed framework from three aspects: convergence speed, model generalization ability and model flexibility.

Rapid Convergence. Our proposed model is trained on the basis of complementary of two single models. By fitting a new model on the remaining residuals between the true label and another model's output to learn what the former

---

[1] https://www.pytorch.org.

model failed to learn, the new model merely needs to learn less content until reaching convergence with relatively faster speed.

Model Generalization. ResFusion is designed under the problem setting with the input of the combination feature matrix F. When GBDT and DeepFM learn separately with the same input, they would focus on different content even in the same data according to their different learning methods. ResFusion's learning ability is no longer single and one-sided, and it can learn the hidden information more generally under the input data. Through the repeated joint learning of two completely different learning mechanisms, the optimal solution of the model can be obtained. So our fusion model finally proves to have better generalization and scalability.

Model Flexibility. ResFusion can also be understood as a result fusion model. Distinguished from other result fusion methods mentioned above, our model doesn't rely on the additional external fusion aggregation model for learning, rather, it's artfully sequentially links the two model as the fuse process during the model training process. So ResFusion can also be extended with feature fusion methods, which highlights the superior flexibility of our model.

In general, distinct from the plain feature fusion models, ResFusion uses the different learning capabilities of the two types of models more directly utilizing both the advantages from the models. Additionally, In our model, the latter (e.g., DeepFM) learns the remaining residual parts based on what the former (e.g., GBDT) has not learned, thus the speed of model convergence will be relatively accelerated. Specially, ResFusion has better generalization ability. Compared with the result fusion models, we fuse two methods naturally as an integral joint learning process and do not depend on the specific external aggregation method. Therefore ResFusion is also very flexible and can also be used in combination with other fusion methods mentioned formerly.

4   Experiments

In this section, we conduct extensive experiments on three real-world datasets to evaluate the effectiveness of our proposed fusion models.

Table 1. The statistics of the three datasets

Dataset	Total instances	Train	Test	Numerical features	Categorical features
Avazu	40 M	36 M	4 M	0	23
Cretio	45 M	40.5 M	4.5 M	13	26
ZhiHu	2 M	1.8 M	0.2 M	131	18

4.1 Experimental Settings

Datasets. To evaluate the effectiveness of our proposed fusion model, we conduct experiments on three public datasets: Avazu, Criteo and ZhiHu datasets:
1) **Avazu.** $Avazu^2$ comes from kaggle CTR prediction competition [12,14]. It consists of 40 M click logs arranged in chronological order along ten days.
2) **Criteo.** $Criteo^3$ as a famous and accessible benchmarking dataset widely used in CTR model evaluation [9,12]. It includes 45 M click records
3) **ZhiHu.** $ZhiHu^4$ derives from ZhiYuan 2019 artificial intelligence competition. The provided data consists of 2M instances of inviting users to answer questions. For the above three datasets, we first filled the null values in numerical features with 0 and categorical features with -1. After data pre-processing, we randomly split all records into train and test with the ratio of 9:1. The number of numerical features and categorical features for different datasets and other detailed dataset statistics are shown in Table 1.

Evaluation Metrics. We adopt two widely used evaluation metrics in experiments: AUC (Area Under ROC) and Logloss(cross entropy). AUC is used to evaluate the probability of ranking positive samples to be front while Logloss is used to measure the difference between predictions and true labels.

Baselines. We compare our proposed model with several state-of-the-art baselines for CTR prediction. We split all baselines into four groups: 1)Traditional machine learning models: LR [20], FM [19] and GBDT [7]; 2) Deep learning based models: DeepFM [9]; 3) Feature fusion models: GBDT+LR [11], GBDT2DNN [18], GBDT2DeepFM [18]; 4) Prediction fusion models: $\overline{GBDT + DeepFM}$ [1].

4.2 Overall Comparisons

In this section, we compare the overall performances of our proposed framework with other baselines. Specifically, Table 2 summarizes the AUC and Logloss values of various models on three datasets. We firstly analyze the single-models: LR only considers each feature's linear combination for CTR prediction, FM exceeds LR by combining the two features and obtaining the information of the second-order cross feature. GBDT can capture effective features and feature linear combinations efficient than LR by combining multiple weak classifiers. DeepFM performs better than FM, showing the effectiveness of the combination of DNN and FM. We find that DeepFM shows a better performance than GBDT on the Avazu dataset but not on the Cretio and ZhiHu datasets. The reason is, as we mentioned before, that shallow model is more suitable for dense numerical

---

[2] https://www.kaggle.com/c/avazu-ctr-prediction.
[3] https://www.kaggle.com/c/criteo-display-ad-challenge.
[4] https://biendata.com/competition/zhihu2019.

Table 2. AUC and Logloss comparisons for different models

Models	Avazu		Cretio		ZhiHu	
	AUC	Logloss	AUC	Logloss	AUC	Logloss
LR	0.5453	0.4554	0.5690	0.5650	0.6122	0.5613
FM	0.7759	0.3820	0.7674	0.5052	0.7319	0.4102
GBDT	0.7608	0.3895	0.8009	0.4495	0.8390	0.3706
DeepFM	0.7852	0.3779	0.7959	0.4569	0.7712	0.3787
GBDT+LR	0.7634	0.3877	0.8025	0.4423	0.8405	0.3700
GBDT2DNN	0.7858	0.3761	0.8031	0.4417	0.8409	0.3699
GBDT2DeepFM	0.7863	0.3741	0.8037	0.4412	0.8417	0.3702
$\overline{GBDT + DeepFM}$	0.7860	0.3767	0.8022	0.4367	0.8411	0.3707
NNres+GBDT	0.7872	0.3726	0.8030	0.4379	0.8420	0.3702
GBDTRes+NN	**0.7921**	**0.3720**	**0.8065**	**0.4348**	**0.8676**	**0.3679**

features and deep model is more suitable for sparse categorical features. Furthermore, we can find the difference on three datasets, the Avazu dataset has only categorical features. Then, we compare our model with other fusion models: for GBDT+LR, we take the output leaf nodes of GBDT as extra feature of data set to feed in LR; GBDT2DNN and GBDT2DeepFM are fed GBDT's predictions as extra features into DNN and DeepFM respectively. The three fusion models fuse GBDT with other models on feature-level and all exceed GBDT. Different from fusion on feature-level, $\overline{GBDT + DeepFM}$ model fuses GBDT and DeepFM on output-level by learning the weight parameters for two outputs for final predictions. Compared with other fusion models, our GBDTRes+NN model which is based on ResFusion framework consistently achieves best performance on both evaluation metrics. On *ZhiHu* dataset, our model improves best fusion baselines by 2.59% and 0.2% on AUC and Logloss, respectively. Based on the analysis of above experimental results, we could empirically conclude that our proposed ResFusion framework outperforms all baselines.

4.3   Detailed Model Analysis

In this subsection, we would like to give a detailed analysis of our proposed ResFusion framework and show the effectiveness of our fusion strategy.

Convergence Speed Analysis. We logged the convergence process of our GBDTRes+NN and other NN (DeepFM)-based models to verify that our model has faster convergence speed. Figure 3 shows the convergence process of AUC and Logloss values on the Avazu dataset. We find that our model achieves convergence at the second epoch. Compared with the deepFM model, which mainly requires nearly six epochs to converge, it is faster by nearly four epochs. Compared with the other two fusion models, our model is also faster by about two epochs. The reason is that our fusion model is based on residual learning, the

DeepFM module only needs to fit the residual part which GBDT did not learn very well, so it can achieve convergence rapidly.

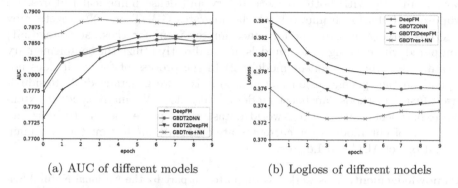

(a) AUC of different models   (b) Logloss of different models

Fig. 3. The convergence speed comparison on various fusion models

Table 3. AUC and Logloss comparisons with different number of iterations K.

Residual iteration	Avazu		Cretio		ZhiHu	
	AUC	Logloss	AUC	Logloss	AUC	Logloss
$K = 0$	0.7608	0.3895	0.8011	0.4495	0.8390	0.3706
$K = 1$	0.7921	0.3720	0.8069	0.4350	0.8676	0.3679
$K = 2$	**0.7925**	**0.3717**	**0.8073**	**0.4341**	**0.8684**	**0.3679**
$K = 3$	0.7922	0.3720	0.8071	0.4351	0.8680	0.3680

Model Generalization Analysis. In this part, We verify the generalization of our proposed framework by setting different number of residual learning K. The experiment results can be observed in Table 3. In the verification experiment, we choose GBDT as the initial model so our fusion model can be seen as a single GBDT model when $K = 0$. Then the results of $K = 1$ mean that we use the DeepFM to fit the residual values of real-labels and the predictions of GBDT, called GBDTRes+NN. The improvement of AUC over the single model (GBDT) is 3.13%. After that, we feed the predictions of the first fusion model GBDTRes+NN's into the GBDT to fit the residual again when $K = 2$. We can do residual learning in an iterative way at different K. According to the experimental results, when $K = 2$, our strategy reaches the best, which means that through the first two residual learning, each model has already fully learned the residual part that another model does not learn. So as K increases to 3 from 2, the performance of the fusion model can no longer be improved, and may even result in over-fitting which leads to suboptimal results.

5   Conclusion

In order to alleviate the challenge that the existing CTR models cannot fully learn from data with both sparse category and dense numerical features, we propose a ResFusion framework which integrates GBDT and NN together by residual learning. It gains performance improvement for these advantages: 1) Compared with existing fusion models, it can directly utilize the complementary advantages of the component models; 2) In the process of fusion, it does not depend on the specific fusion method, so it is more generalized; 3) Residual-based fusion methods can boost model convergence. We finally conduct extensive experiments on three real-world datasets and prove the effectiveness and efficiency of our model over current state-of-the-art models on the two main evaluations of AUC and Logloss.

Acknowledgement. This work was supported in part by the National Natural Science Foundation of China (Grant No. 61972125, U19A2079), the Fundamental Research Funds for the Central Universities (Grant No. JZ2020HGPA0114), Zhejiang Lab (No. 2019KE0AB04) and the Foundation of Key Laboratory of Cognitive Intelligence, iFLYTEK, P.R., China (Grant No. COGOS-20190002).

References

1. Abedalla, A., et al.: MTRecS-DLT: multi-modal transport recommender system using deep learning and tree models. In: 2019 SNAMS, pp. 274–278. IEEE (2019). https://doi.org/10.1109/SNAMS.2019.8931864
2. Chen, L., Wu, L., Hong, R., Zhang, K., Wang, M.: Revisiting graph based collaborative filtering: a linear residual graph convolutional network approach. In: AAAI2020, vol. 34, pp. 27–34 (2020)
3. Chen, T., Guestrin, C.: XGBoost: a scalable tree boosting system. In: KDD2016, KDD 2016, p. 785–794. Association for Computing Machinery, New York (2016). https://doi.org/10.1145/2939672.2939785
4. Cheng, H., Cantú-Paz, E.: Personalized click prediction in sponsored search. In: WSDM (2010). https://doi.org/10.1145/1718487.1718531
5. Cheng, H.T., et al.: Wide & deep learning for recommender systems. https://doi.org/10.1145/2988450.2988454
6. Freund, Y., Schapire, R.E.: A decision-theoretic generalization of on-line learning and an application to boosting. In: Proceedings of the Second European Conferenceon Computational Learning Theory (1995). https://doi.org/10.1006/jcss.1997.1504
7. Friedman, J.H.: Greedy function approximation: a gradient boosting machine. Ann. Stat., 1189–1232 (2001). https://doi.org/10.1214/aos/1013203451
8. Graepel, T., Borchert, T., Herbrich, R.: Web-scale Bayesian click-through rate prediction for sponsored search advertising in microsoft's bing search engine (2010). https://doi.org/10.5555/3104322.3104326
9. Guo, H., Tang, R., Ye, Y., Li, Z., He, X.: DeepFM: a factorization-machine based neural network for CTR prediction. https://doi.org/10.24963/ijcai.2017/239
10. He, K., Zhang, X., Ren, S., Sun, J.: Deep residual learning for image recognition. In: CVPR, pp. 770–778 (2016). https://doi.org/10.1109/CVPR.2016.90

11. He, X., et al.: Practical lessons from predicting clicks on ads at facebook. In: Proceedings of the Eighth International Workshop on Data Mining for Online Advertising, pp. 1–9 (2014). https://doi.org/10.1145/2648584.2648589

12. Huang, T., Zhang, Z., Zhang, J.: FiBiNET: combining feature importance and bilinear feature interaction for click-through rate prediction. In: Proceedings of the 13th ACM Conference on Recommender Systems, pp. 169–177 (2019). https://doi.org/10.1145/3298689.3347043

13. Juan, Y., Lefortier, D., Chapelle, O.: Field-aware factorization machines in a real-world online advertising system. In: Proceedings of the 26th International Conference on World Wide Web Companion, pp. 680–688 (2017). https://doi.org/10.1145/3041021.3054185

14. Juan, Y., Zhuang, Y., Chin, W.S., Lin, C.J.: Field-aware factorization machines for CTR prediction. In: Proceedings of the 10th ACM Conference on Recommender Systems, pp. 43–50 (2016). https://doi.org/10.1145/2959100.2959134

15. Ke, G., et al.: LightGBM: a highly efficient gradient boosting decision tree. In: Advances In Neural Information Processing Systems, pp. 3146–3154 (2017). https://doi.org/10.5555/3294996.3295074

16. Ke, G., Xu, Z., Zhang, J., Bian, J., Liu, T.Y.: DeepGBM: a deep learning framework distilled by GBDT for online prediction tasks. In: Proceedings of the 25th ACM SIGKDD International Conference on Knowledge Discovery & Data Mining, pp. 384–394 (2019). https://doi.org/10.1145/3292500.3330858

17. Lian, J., Zhou, X., Zhang, F., Chen, Z., Xie, X., Sun, G.: xDeepFM: combining explicit and implicit feature interactions for recommender systems. https://doi.org/10.1145/3219819.3220023

18. Ling, X., Deng, W., Chen, G., Zhou, H., Cui, L., Feng, S.: Model ensemble for click prediction in bing search ads (2017). https://doi.org/10.1145/3041021.3054192

19. Rendle, S.: Factorization machines. In: 2010 IEEE International Conference on Data Mining, pp. 995–1000. IEEE (2010). https://doi.org/10.1109/ICDM.2010.127

20. Richardson, M., Dominowska, E., Ragno, R.: Predicting clicks: estimating the click-through rate for new ads. In: Proceedings of the 16th International Conference on World Wide Web, pp. 521–530 (2007). https://doi.org/10.1145/1242572.1242643

21. Trofimov, I., Kornetova, A., Topinskiy, V.: Using boosted trees for click-through rate prediction for sponsored search. In: Data Mining for Online Advertising and Internet Economy, pp. 1–6 (2012)

22. Wang, R., Fu, B., Fu, G., Wang, M.: Deep & cross network for ad click predictions. https://doi.org/10.1145/3124749.3124754

23. Wu, L., Sun, P., Fu, Y., Hong, R., Wang, X., Wang, M.: A neural influence diffusion model for social recommendation. In: SIGIR2019, pp. 235–244 (2019)

24. Yang, A.: A recommendation system based on fusing boosting model and DNN model. https://doi.org/10.32604/cmc.2019.07704

25. YuChin Juan, W.S.C., Zhuang, Y.: 3 Idiots' Approach for Display Advertising Challenge (2014). https://github.com/ycjuan/kaggle-2014-criteo/

NLP for IR

A Framework for Identifying Event's Relevance Comments in Twitter

Darong Peng[1], Nankai Lin[1], Xiaotian Lin[1], Xubin Yan[1],
and Shengyi Jiang[1,2(✉)]

[1] School of Information Science and Technology, Guangdong University
of Foreign Studies, Guangzhou, China
jiangshengyi@163.com
[2] Guangzhou Key Laboratory of Multilingual Intelligent Processing,
Guangdong University of Foreign Studies, Guangzhou, China

Abstract. Nowadays, with the continuous development of the Internet, public opinion analysis has become an indispensable means for governments and companies to grasp public opinion trends and respond promptly to emergencies. Finding out a topic's relevant comments is more conducive to providing analysis foundation. Twitter, a popular social media website, permits users to post their viewpoints about an event. An event's relevant comments could be obtained through twitter search using the event's key phrases. However, twitter search utilizes the full-match mode, which the search results contain a large number of irrelevant comments for it doesn't use a correlation filter. In this paper, we proposed a framework for identifying twitter relevance comments (ITRC). The framework treats ITRC as a text matching task and matches one comment with all news of an event to distinguish whether the comment is a relevance comment in twitter. Before the matching module, we adopted the Rake algorithm to extract key phrases from the event's news and then the key phrases were used for twitter search to construct twitter relevant comments dataset. Based on this dataset, the effectiveness of different text matching methods was examined. Through the in-event and cross-event experiments, we used the MV-LSTM with the best overall performance as our matching module. Moreover, we also mixed data from different events to conduct the experiments. The experimental results demonstrated the effectiveness of the mixed data strategy.

Keywords: Text matching · Identify twitter relevance comments · Key phrases extraction

1 Introduction

With the advent of the Web 3.0 era, personal user information and published information play a particularly important role on the Internet. Twitter, a social internet service in the internet epoch, has become a popular platform for information sharing and communication, whose users have been over 500 million, publishing over 200

D. Peng and N. Lin are co-first authors of the article.

© Springer Nature Switzerland AG 2020
Z. Dou et al. (Eds.): CCIR 2020, LNCS 12285, pp. 45–57, 2020.
https://doi.org/10.1007/978-3-030-56725-5_4

million, which contain crucial information. Nowadays, the current research on twitter text mainly concentrates on spam text detection [1], high-quality recommendation of twitter content [2], emotion classification from twitter text [3] and twitter rumor detection [4]. Instead, it's extremely rare for researchers to dig twitter comments concerning hot events, which turns out to be of great practical significance. Identifying the twitter comments concerned to hot events is not only extraordinarily valuable for grasping the dynamic trend of public opinion, offering appropriate public opinion guidance and providing basis for analysis, but also beneficial for the governments and enterprises to make reasonable strategies by extension according to the public opinion trend of that event. In the meanwhile, identifying relative comments enables judicial trial to master public opinion analysis from different angles, which is more conducive for the government to supervise the judiciary and facilitating the progress of judicature.

In this paper, we constructed a twitter relevant comments dataset which contains three events' relevant comments. The three events are the arrest of Meng Wanzhou, British truck carrying corpse case and Trump's impeachment. The dataset of each event contains 10 news related to the event, event's key phrases and twitter relevant comments marked with relevance. Moreover, we proposed a framework for identifying twitter relevance comments (ITRC). The framework treats ITRC as a text matching task and matches one comment with all news of an event to distinguish whether the comment is a relevance comment in twitter. The ITRC is divided into two stages, prescreening the relevance comments and identifying the relevance comments. The MV-LSTM, Match-Pyramid, ESIM, and Pair-CNN algorithms were used as the matching module in the framework. We respectively used the single event data and the mixed data to conduct experiments, and compared the performance of our model on in-event experiment and cross-event experiment.

In summary, the contributions of this paper are: (1) we constructed a twitter relevant comments dataset which contains three events' twitter relevant comments; (2) we proposed a framework for identifying twitter relevance comments (ITRC); (3) we verified the performance and effectiveness of each module in our framework; (4) we explored the structure of the matching module with the best performance among the framework; (5) we verified that using the data containing multiple events as the training set to conduct the experiment can preferably improve the model performance on cross-event data.

2   Related Work

2.1   Identifying Event's Relevance Comments

At present, domestic and foreign research working on the quality of Twitter texts and the relevance of various social media texts is scarce, but the rapid identification of event-related Twitter texts has very important practical significance and value.

Krestel et al. devise generic techniques to recommend tweets for any given news article [5]. To evaluate and compare the different techniques, they collected tens of thousands of tweets and news articles and conducted a user study on the relevance of recommendations. Liu's research on whether Weibo comments are related to the body of text [6] mainly focuses on the semantic similarity of text and the behavior of users themselves. Becker et al. explored approaches for finding representative messages among a set of twitter messages that correspond to the same event, with the goal of identifying high quality, relevant messages that provide useful event information [7]. Yang et al. present a spectrum of topic modeling techniques that contribute to a deployed system which includes non-topical tweet detection, automatic labeled data acquisition, evaluation with human computation, diagnostic and corrective learning and high-precision topic inference [8].

2.2 Text Matching

Text matching is a core problem in natural language understanding. The research on text matching can be applied to a large number of known natural language processing tasks, such as information retrieval, automatic question answering, machine translation, dialogue systems, paraphrase identification, and so on. These natural language processing tasks can be abstracted into text matching problems to a certain extent. For example, information retrieval can be reduced to the matching of query terms and documents. Yang et al. proposed a learning framework that leverages external knowledge for response ranking in information-seeking conversation systems [9]. In addition, automatic question answering can be simplified to the matching of questions and candidate answers. Chen et al. presented the design of Multi-Channel Information Crossing (MIX), a multi-channel convolutional neural network (CNN) model for text matching in automatic question answering task, with additional attention mechanisms on sentences and semantic features [10]. Machine translation can be considered as the matching of two languages. What's more, the dialogue system could be simplified to the matching of the previous sentence as well as the reply and the paraphrasing problem could be simplified to the matching of the two synonyms.

3 Method

3.1 ITRC Framework

As shown in Fig. 1, the ITRC is divided into two stages, prescreening the relevance comments and identifying the relevance comments.

While prescreening the relevance comments, firstly, our framework crawls the news about events on the BBC News[1] as the text representation of the event, and afterwards uses the Rake algorithm to extract key phrases from the news event titles. In this paper, we obtain ten news for each event to conduct experiments. Based on the threshold of the key phrase we set, we filtered out the set containing key phrases for searching. Then the key phrases were used for twitter search to prescreen the relevance comments.

In the relevance comments identification module, we treat ITRC as a text matching task and match one comment with all news of an event to distinguish whether the comment is a relevance comment in twitter. In this paper, the MV-LSTM,

---

[1] https://www.bbc.co.uk/news.

Match-Pyramid, ESIM, and PairCNN algorithms were used to match the news text with the tweet comments, and identify the twitter text whether related to the event. In the text matching phase, we calculated the correlation between the tweet text and the ten news texts. If there is news related to the tweet comment, the twitter comment is considered to be related to the event.

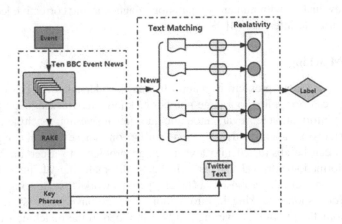

Fig. 1. The ITRC framework

3.2 Rake

The Rake algorithm [11] is used for keyword extraction. Actually, it extracts key phrases and tends to longer phrases. In English, key phrases usually include multiple words, but rarely include punctuation, stop words and other words that do not contain semantic information.

In this paper, we regarded the ten news of an event as an event document collection. The Rake algorithm first divides a document into several clauses by punctuation (such as periods, question marks, exclamation marks, commas, etc.), and then for each clause, the stop words are used as a separator to divide the clause into several phrases, and these phrases are regarded as the candidate phrases. Then, the candidate phrases are constructed into a co-occurrence matrix, and the frequency and the degree of these candidate phrases are extracted. The ratio of degree to frequency is used as the score of the candidate phrases, the formula is as follows:

$$Score = Degree(w) \div Frequency(w) \tag{1}$$

After feature extraction, we initially merge the keywords that adjoin one another at least twice with the same order in the same document to become a new candidate key phrase. The score for the new candidate words is the sum of its member key phrases' scores. Eventually, through arranging the score of the candidate key phrases with descending order, we can elect the first n candidate keywords outputted as the key phrases of the event.

3.3 Text Matching Algorithm

MV-LSTM is a text matching model proposed by Wan et al. [12], which is a multi-semantic model based on a Bi-LSTM network. The structure of the model is shown in Fig. 2. MV-LSTM model uses Bi-LSTM to process the news and comment, and then calculates the matching degree of the output of the hidden layers of Bi-LSTM, which is called multi-View (MV) process. Using Bi-LSTM to process sentences at the same time is equivalent to interpreting sentences step-by-step with a variable-length window, which achieves the effect of examining sentences with multiple granularities.

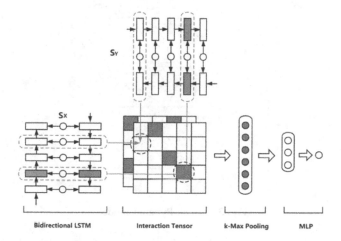

Fig. 2. MV-LSTM model

Firstly, the model uses Bi-LSTM model to generate each positional sentence representation of news and comments, and then uses the tensor layer to model interactions between two vectors. The tensor layer is as follows:

$$s(u, v) = f\left(u^T M^{[1:c]} v + W_{uv} \begin{bmatrix} u \\ v \end{bmatrix} + b\right) \tag{2}$$

where v, u respectively represent two vectors, and M^i ($i \in [1, \ldots, c]$) is one slice of the tensor. W_{uv} and b are the parameters of the linear transformation. f is a non-linear function and the result after the tensor function transformation is a interaction tensor.

Next, k-Max sampling is used to select the k-largest values from each slice of the interactive tensor, and then the values of all slices are stitched into a vector. The final matching score is produced by aggregating such interactions through a multilayer perceptron. The formula is as follows:

$$r = f(W_r q + b_r) \tag{3}$$

$$s = W_s r + b_s \tag{4}$$

where W_r and W_s are parameter matrices, and b_r and b_s are corresponding biases.

Match-Pyramid is proposed by Liang Pang et al. [13]. The model structure is shown in Fig. 3. The model firstly converts the text sequence data into a similarity matrix. In this paper, the cosine distance is used to construct the matching matrix. Based on the matching matrix, Match-Pyramid conducts hierarchical convolution to extract matching patterns. After hierarchical convolution, two additional fully connected layers are used to aggregate the information into a single matching score.

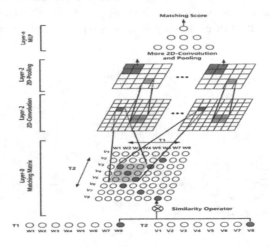

Fig. 3. Match-Pyramid model

ESIM was proposed by Chen et al. [14]. The structure of the model is shown in Fig. 4. It is used for natural language inference, and is used for related tasks of text matching after a little modification. The objective of its loss function is to estimate whether two sequences are synonymous sentences or not. The ESIM model structure is divided into four parts: input encoding, local inference modeling, inference composition, and prediction.

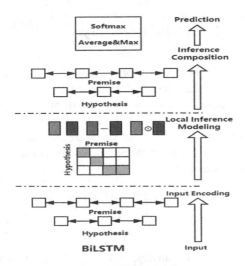

Fig. 4. ESIM model

Input Encoding: The input of this layer can generally use pre-trained word vectors or use an embedding layer, then use Bi-LSTM to encode local inference information and its interaction. $\bar{a}_i$ and $\bar{b}_j$ are the hidden (output) state generated by the Bi-LSTM at time i or j over the input sequence a or b.

$$\bar{a}_i = BiLSTM(a, i), i \in (1, \ldots, l_a) \tag{5}$$

$$\bar{b}_j = BiLSTM(b, j), j \in (1, \ldots, l_b) \tag{6}$$

Local Inference Modeling: This layer is used to calculate the difference between the feature values obtained in the input layer, and calculate the similarity of each word between the two sequences:

$$e_{ij} = \bar{a}_i^T \bar{b}_j \tag{7}$$

A two-dimensional similarity matrix is obtained, where e_{ij} is the similarity between the words $\bar{a}_i$ and $\bar{b}_j$. And then e_{ij} is combined with $\bar{a}_i$, $\bar{b}_j$ to generates sentences weighted by the similarity between each other.

$$\tilde{a}_i = \sum_{j=1}^{l_b} \frac{\exp(e_{ij})}{\sum_{k=1}^{l_b} \exp(e_{ik})} \bar{b}_j, i \in (1, \ldots, l_a) \tag{8}$$

$$\tilde{b}_j = \sum_{i=1}^{l_a} \frac{\exp(e_{ij})}{\sum_{k=1}^{l_a} \exp(e_{kj})} \bar{a}_i, j \in (1, \ldots, l_b) \tag{9}$$

After obtaining the encoding value and the weighted encoding value, ESIM performs a difference calculation between with these two values, and concentrates the values of the two states of encoding with the subtracted and multiplied values:

$$m_a = (\bar{a}; \tilde{a}; \bar{a} - \tilde{a}; \bar{a} \odot \tilde{a}) \tag{10}$$

$$m_b = (\bar{b}; \tilde{b}; \bar{b} - \tilde{b}; \bar{b} \odot \tilde{b}) \tag{11}$$

Inference Composition: This layer uses Bi-LSTM for feature extraction of m_a, m_b, which is mainly used to capture the local inference information m_a and m_b and their context for inference composition. Ultimately, we respectively apply a maximum pooling operation and an average pooling operation to pool the vectors obtained by BI-LSTM and concatenate the vectors pooled afterwards.

$$V_{a,ave} = \sum_{i=1}^{l_a} \frac{V_{a,i}}{l_a}, V_{a,max} = max_{i=1}^{l_a} V_{a,i} \tag{12}$$

$$V_{b,ave} = \sum_{j=1}^{l_b} \frac{V_{b,j}}{l_b}, V_{b,max} = max_{j=1}^{l_b} V_{b,j} \tag{13}$$

$$V = \left[V_{a,ave}; V_{a,max}; V_{b,ave}; V_{b,max}\right] \tag{14}$$

Prediction: Finally, V is fed to the fully connected layer. The activation function uses the tanh function, and the result is fed to the softmax layer for classification.

Pair-CNN is a convolutional neural network architecture proposed by Severyn et al. [15], which is shown in Fig. 5. The network requires minimal preprocessing. The input of the network are raw words that need to be translated into real-valued feature vectors to be processed by subsequent layers of the network. The convolution layer and the pooling layer are used for feature extraction of news and comment. Then the distributional representations of a piece of news x_q and a comment x_d are obtained by the convolution layer and the pooling layer are used to compute a news-comment similarity score. The formula is as follows:

$$sim\left(x_{q,}, x_d\right) = x_q^T M x_d \tag{15}$$

where $M \in R^{d*d}$ is a similarity matrix. The model concatenates the similarity score and the distributional representations of a piece of news x_q and a document x_d, and then passed through a fully connected hidden layer. Finally the output vector from the fully connected hidden layer is fed to a softmax classification layer.

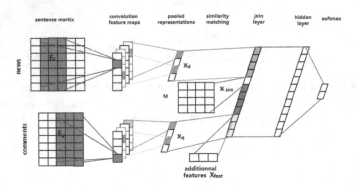

Fig. 5. Pair-CNN model

4   Data and Metric

We construct a twitter relevant comments dataset which contains three events' twitter relevant comments. The three events are the arrest of Meng Wanzhou (event 1), British truck carrying corpse case (event 2) and Trump's impeachment (event 3). The dataset of each event contains 10 news related to the event, event's key phrases and twitter relevant comments marked with relevance. Table 1 shows that the distributions of comments' relevance for each event. For each event, the data were divided into the training dataset (80%), the validation dataset (10%) and the testing dataset (10%).

Table 1. The distributions of comments' relevance for each event

Event	Related	Not related	Total
The arrest of Meng Wanzhou	4288	2514	6802
British truck carrying corpse case	1700	2722	4422
Trump's impeachment	5507	4205	9712

In this paper, the accuracy and F_1 values were applied to evaluate the results. Using accuracy as a measurement index can evaluate whether the classification of the framework can do a good job in terms of relevance. The value of F_1 which adequately takes the accuracy and the recall rate into account can comprehensively measure the performance of the framework.

5   Result and Analysis

5.1   Key Phrase Screening Threshold Determination

In the key phrase extraction phase, the parameters of the Rake algorithm are shown in Table 2.

Table 2. The parameters of the Rake algorithm

Parameters	Value	Explanation
min_char_length	5	The minimum number of characters in key phrases
max_words_length	3	The maximum number of words in a phrase
min_words_length_adj	0	The minimum number of adjectives in key phrases
max_words_length_adj	1	The maximum number of adjectives in key phrases
min_keyword_frequency	1	The minimum frequency of key phrases

In order to ascertain the threshold for filtering keywords in the prescreening the relevance comments module, we calculated the proportion of relevant comments in the three events and the threshold of the phrase number filtered the key words by means of Rake algorithm. The experimental results are shown in Fig. 6. It is obvious to see that the number of keywords is 6 when the proportion of the relevance comments is the highest or shows a clear downward trend. Therefore, the optimal threshold to filter the keywords in the framework's prescreening the relevance comments module is 6.

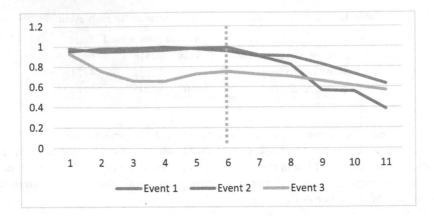

Fig. 6. The distribution of relevance comments

5.2 Unmixed Data Experiments

In this experiment, we use the correlation classification performance of a single event in this event and the classification performance of two other events to conduct experiments, and mix two events to conduct training tests to test the classification performance of this model in the third category of events. In the experiment, the accuracy and F_1 value are used as the evaluation criteria.

We utilize the training set of one event for training and verify the effect of the test set on the original event and the other two events as well, which is shown from Table 3, Table 4 and Table 5. In these three experiments, the F_1 values of the MV-LSTM model are 0.9502, 0.9652 and 0.8569 respectively, whose performance outperform other models on the original event. Simultaneously, in the cross-event experiments, although the Match-Pyramid model performs best in the first experiment, the MV-LSTM model has achieved good results in the other two experiments. Therefore, we determine to utilize the MV-LSTM model which has the best performance based on the above experimental results as the model of our identifying relevance module.

Table 3. The experiment that uses training data of Event 1

Model	Event					
	Event 1		Event 2		Event 3	
	Accuracy	F_1	Accuracy	F_1	Accuracy	F_1
MV-LSTM	**0.9504**	**0.9502**	0.5326	0.5201	0.5880	0.5313
Match-Pyramid	0.8020	0.7932	**0.6580**	**0.5222**	**0.7233**	**0.6833**
ESIM	0.9021	0.8938	0.4932	0.4870	0.5462	0.5210
Pair-CNN	0.7620	0.7724	0.3346	0.3182	0.5016	0.5134

Table 4. The experiment that uses training data of Event 2

Model	Event					
	Event 2		Event 1		Event 3	
	Accuracy	F_1	Accuracy	F_1	Accuracy	F_1
MV-LSTM	**0.9651**	**0.9652**	**0.5546**	**0.5190**	0.6151	**0.5347**
Match-Pyramid	0.7324	0.7900	0.4413	0.3002	**0.6282**	0.4847
ESIM	0.8634	0.8402	0.5214	0.4607	0.5847	0.5743
Pair-CNN	0.8127	0.7833	0.4031	0.4021	0.4857	0.4472

Table 5. The experiment that uses training data of Event 3

Model	Event					
	Event 3		Event 1		Event 2	
	Accuracy	F_1	Accuracy	F_1	Accuracy	F_1
MV-LSTM	**0.8566**	**0.8569**	0.4181	0.4001	0.5622	**0.5720**
Match Pyramid	0.6364	0.4949	0.4413	0.2802	**0.6580**	0.5222
ESIM	0.6978	0.6324	**0.4673**	**0.4345**	0.5279	0.5190
Pair-CNN	0.7014	0.6745	0.3987	0.3591	0.4671	0.4670

5.3 Mixed Data Experiments

We further utilize the mixed data containing the events of Meng Wanzhou and UK truck carrying corpses as the training set to conduct the experiment whose result is shown in Table 6. Palpably, the MV-LSTM models still outperform the others while the F_1 value in the other event achieves the highest as well. In addition, we verify the performance of unmixed data operation as well as mixed data operation with the Trump's impeachment event. The result is shown in Table 7. It is obvious to see that using the data mixed with multiple events as the training set to conduct the experiment can preferably improve the model performance on cross-event data.

Table 6. The experiment that uses training data of Event 1 and Event 2

Model	Event			
	Event 1 and Event 2		Event 3	
	Accuracy	F_1	Accuracy	F_1
MV-LSTM	**0.9685**	**0.9685**	0.5825	**0.5712**
Match-Pyramid	0.8279	0.8148	**0.6282**	0.4847
ESIM	0.8358	0.8032	0.5982	0.5345
Pair-CNN	0.8562	0.8204	0.6002	0.5927

Table 7. The results of different experiments in Event 3

Model	Event	
	Event 3	
	Accuracy	F_1
MV-LSTM with unmixed data	**0.5880**	0.5313
MV-LSTM with mixed data	0.5825	**0.5712**

6   Conclusion

In this paper, we proposed a framework for identifying twitter relevance comments. We respectively used the single event data and the mixed data to conduct experiments, and compared the performance of our model on in-event experiment and cross-event experiment. The framework we construct performs relatively well on in-event experiment while on cross-event data its performance still needs enhancement. At the same time, using the data mixed with different events as the training set to train our framework could improve the performance of the model on cross-event data. In the future, we will augment the scale of the dataset making it contain more events so as to further explore how to preferably improve the model's performance on cross-event.

Acknowledgement. This work was supported by the National Natural Science Foundation of China (No. 61572145), the Major Projects of Guangdong Education Department for Foundation Research and Applied Research (No. 2017KZDXM031) and National Social Science Foundation of China (No. 17CTQ045). The authors would like to thank the anonymous reviewers for their valuable comments and suggestions.

References

1. Wu, T., Liu, S., Zhang, J., Xiang, Y.: Twitter spam detection based on deep learning. In: ACM International Conference Proceeding Series (2017). https://doi.org/10.1145/3014812.3014815
2. Chen, K., Chen, T., Zheng, G., Jin, O., Yao, E., Yu, Y.: Collaborative personalized tweet recommendation. In: SIGIR 2012 - Proceedings of the International ACM SIGIR Conference on Research and Development in Information Retrieval (2012). https://doi.org/10.1145/2348283.2348372
3. Lakomkin, E., Bothe, C., Wermter, S.: GradAscent at EmoInt-2017: Character and Word Level Recurrent Neural Network Models for Tweet Emotion Intensity Detection. presented at the (2018). https://doi.org/10.18653/v1/w17-5222
4. Takahashi, T., Igata, N.: Rumor detection on twitter. In: 6th International Conference on Soft Computing and Intelligent Systems, and 13th International Symposium on Advanced Intelligence Systems, SCIS/ISIS 2012 (2012). https://doi.org/10.1109/SCIS-ISIS.2012.6505254
5. Krestel, R., Werkmeister, T., Wiradarma, T.P., Kasneci, G.: Tweet-recommender: finding relevant tweets for news articles. In: WWW 2015 Companion - Proceedings of the 24th International Conference on World Wide Web (2015). https://doi.org/10.1145/2740908.2742716

6. Liu, Z.: Research on the relevance of Chinese Weibo reviews and Weibo topics (2016)
7. Becker, H., Gravano, L.: Selecting quality Twitter content for events. In: International AAAI Conference on Weblogs Social Media (2010)
8. Yang, S.H., Kolcz, A., Schlaikjer, A., Gupta, P.: Large-scale high-precision topic modeling on Twitter. In: Proceedings of the ACM SIGKDD International Conference on Knowledge Discovery and Data Mining (2014). https://doi.org/10.1145/2623330.2623336
9. Yang, L., et al.: Response ranking with deep matching networks and external knowledge in information-seeking conversation systems. In: 41st International ACM SIGIR Conference on Research and Development in Information Retrieval, SIGIR 2018 (2018). https://doi.org/10.1145/3209978.3210011
10. Chen, H., Liu, D., Han, F.X., Lai, K., Xu, Y., Niu, D., Wu, C.: MIX: multi-channel information crossing for text matching. In: Proceedings of the ACM SIGKDD International Conference on Knowledge Discovery and Data Mining (2018). https://doi.org/10.1145/3219819.3219928
11. Rose, S.J., Cowley, W.E., Crow, V.L., Cramer, N.O.: Rapid automatic keyword extraction for information retrieval and analysis (2012)
12. Wan, S., Lan, Y., Guo, J., Xu, J., Pang, L., Cheng, X.: A deep architecture for semantic matching with multiple positional sentence representations. In: 30th AAAI Conference on Artificial Intelligence, AAAI 2016 (2016)
13. Pang, L., Lan, Y., Guo, J., Xu, J., Cheng, X.: A study of MatchPyramid models on ad-hoc retrieval. CoRR. abs/1606.04648 (2016)
14. Chen, Q., Ling, Z., Jiang, H., Zhu, X., Wei, S., Inkpen, D.: Enhanced LSTM for natural language inference. In: ACL 2017 - 55th Annual Meeting of the Association for Computational Linguistics, Proceedings of the Conference (Long Papers) (2017). https://doi.org/10.18653/v1/P17-1152
15. Severyn, A., Moschittiy, A.: Learning to rank short text pairs with convolutional deep neural networks. In: SIGIR 2015 - Proceedings of the 38th International ACM SIGIR Conference on Research and Development in Information Retrieval (2015). https://doi.org/10.1145/2766462.2767738

Enriching Pre-trained Language Model with Dependency Syntactic Information for Chemical-Protein Interaction Extraction

Jianye Fan, Xiaofeng Liu, Shoubin Dong[✉], and Jinlong Hu

Communication and Computer Network Key Laboratory of Guangdong,
School of Computer Science and Engineering,
South China University of Technology, Guangzhou, China
sbdong@scut.edu.cn

Abstract. Automatic extraction of chemical-protein interactions (CPI) included in biomedical literature plays an important role in many biomedical applications such as drug discovery, knowledge discovery, and biomedical knowledge graph construction. However, CPIs in long and complicated sentences are difficult to extract. Most of the existing methods mainly focus on the sequence information rather than syntactic information, which is also conducive to CPI extraction. In this paper, a pre-trained language model based approach with dependency syntactic information is proposed to improve the performance of CPI extraction. Firstly the approach extracts generalized dependency syntactic information based on the characteristics of CPI data. Then, BERT is adopted to generate the contextual representation of sequence information and syntactic information and the mean-pooling method is used to aggregate the context representation. Finally, the sequence information and syntactic information are fused and mapped to the category feature space through a fully-connected layer. The evaluation on the original ChemProt corpus demonstrates that in comparison to other pre-trained model-based methods, our method can achieve better performance.

Keywords: CPI extraction · Pre-trained language model · Dependency syntactic information · BERT

1 Introduction

Automatic extraction of chemical-protein interaction (CPI) plays an important role in many biomedical applications such as drug discovery, knowledge discovery, etc. [1] To date, the exponentially growing biomedical literature has become a storehouse of CPI knowledge. However, confronted with a large amount of biomedical literature, researchers can hardly obtain useful information on their own. Thus automatically extracting CPI described in biomedical literature has become an essential task in biomedical natural language processing (NLP).

In present, most CPI extraction methods can be categorized into machine learning-based methods and neural network-based methods. Machine learning-based methods usually utilize kernel function and feature engineering to learn CPI knowledge.

Z. Dou et al. (Eds.): CCIR 2020, LNCS 12285, pp. 58–69, 2020.
https://doi.org/10.1007/978-3-030-56725-5_5

For example, Lung et al. [2] constructed chemical-protein relation pairs and triplets, as well as complex feature to implement their machine learning method, which achieved certain effect on CPI extraction. But machine learning-based methods are limited by the selection of features, while neural network-based methods can automatically learn potential features. Therefore, neural network-based methods have gradually become the mainstream method of CPI extraction. Corbett et al. [3] introduce the Bi-LSTM model with pre-trained LSTM layer to extract CPI; Peng et al. [4] proposed an ensemble method, which manages the CPI extraction with ensembles of SVM, CNN, and Bi-LSTM models. Both of them can provide relatively good performance. With the development of pre-trained language model, more and more pre-trained model-based methods are applied to CPI extraction. Lee et al. [5] proposed BioBERT, a pre-trained model for biomedical named entity recognition, relation extraction, and question answering. Sun et al. [6] introduced Gaussian probability distribution and external biomedical knowledge into the pre-trained model. Because of the excellent Transformers bidirectional encoder [7] and a large amount of pre-training data, these pre-trained model-based methods can achieve state-of-the-art performances of CPI extraction.

However, the research on CPI extraction is just in its infancy and the performance still has much room for improvement. A big challenge in CPI extraction is how to accurately extract CPI in long and complicated sentences. The chemical and protein entities are often found in different clauses. It is hard to capture the distinguished relation for most existing models in these long and complicated sentences [8]. Besides, the state-of-the-art methods of CPI extraction mainly focus on the sequence features instead of syntactic features. As Phu et al. [9] concluded in their paper, although the attention heads of BERT [10] can track specialist dependency types, their method can not support the existence of generalist heads that can perform holistic parsing. Therefore, we hope to further improve the performance of CPI extraction by integrating dependency syntactic information into pre-trained model. On one hand, it is necessary to develop an appropriate syntactic information extraction method. On the other hand, we need to effectively integrate syntactic information into pre-trained model.

In this paper, a pre-trained language model-based method with integrated dependency syntactic information is proposed to improve the performance of CPI extraction. Firstly a unique syntactic extraction method is designed to capture the generalized dependency syntactic information. Then the syntactic information and the sequence information would be input into BERT, generating sequence contextual representation and syntactic contextual representation. Finally, the two parts are fused and fed into the softmax layer to obtain the CPI relation. In conclusion, this paper has the following contributions:

1) An appropriate syntactic information extraction method is proposed to acquire more generalized dependency syntactic information of complicated sentences.
2) We enrich the pre-trained language model with dependency syntactic information for chemical-protein interaction extraction. The experiments on the ChemProt corpus demonstrate the better performance of our method.

2   Approach

2.1   Model Architecture

Figure 1 is a schematic overview of our proposed model. In general, our model consists of three parts: extraction of syntactic information, BERT representations, and the fusion of sequence and syntactic information. In the beginning, the generalized dependency syntactic information would be extracted as complementary input of pre-trained model. The sequence contextual representations and syntactic contextual representations are then generated by BERT's Transformer encoder. In the fusion component, the output of CLS and ENTITY-MARKER in sequence information would be merged with the output of syntactic information in mean-pooling operation. With a fully-connected layer and softmax layer, the final prediction result can be obtained.

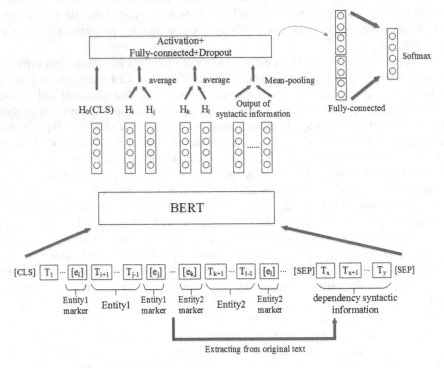

Fig. 1.   Overview of our model.

2.2   Extraction of Dependency Syntactic Information

In our method, it is needed to extract the dependency syntactic information of CPI data. One common approach to leverage syntactic information in relation extraction is to perform bottom-up or top-down computation along the parse tree or the subtree below the lowest common ancestor (LCA) of the entities [11]. Another common approach is to apply a novel pruning strategy to the parse tree by keeping words immediately around the shortest path between the two entities [12]. Nevertheless, the above methods may not be suitable for some complicated sentences. Such as the example shown in Fig. 2, two entities '@CHEM-GENE$' are overlapping, thus the LCA of the entities is non-existent.

23468099.T1.T13----Effects of chronic social defeat stress on behavior and @CHEM-GENE$, 78-kDa glucose-regulated protein, and CCAAT/ enhancer-binding protein (C/EBP) homologous protein in adult mice.----False
17199504.T11.T16----Configuration of a scintillation proximity assay for the activity assessment of recombinant @CHEM-GENE$.----False

Fig. 2. examples of the overlapping entities.

Also, some samples belong to document-level relation extraction, in which the two entities are located in two different sentences. In this case, several parse trees would be generated and it is impossible to directly acquire the shortest path between the two entities. As for our research of some complicated sentences in CPI data, the subtree below LCA of the entities also contains some noise nodes and the shortest path between the entity and the root node also contains some nonnegligible information. As a consequence, our strategy is to apply a pruning strategy to the parse tree by keeping words around the shortest path between the entity node and the root node. More concretely, our extraction method can be described as Algorithm 1.

Algorithm 1: Extraction of dependency syntactic information	
Input:	Text sequence S, entities e1 and e2
Output:	Words set {W}, containing the dependency syntactic information
1:	$S \leftarrow$ Replace(e1, e2) //replace entities in the sentence S with $CHEMICAL$ or $GENE$ or @CHEM-GENE$
2:	Spacy.load() //load model into spacy for parsing
3:	*Parse trees* $\leftarrow$ spacy.nlp(S) //parse the sentence S
4:	**If** entities are overlapping **then**
5:	$W \leftarrow$ put the words around the shortest path between overlapping entity and root node into {W}
6:	**Else if** entities are located in two different sentences **then**
7:	*{path1, path2}* $\leftarrow$ take the two shortest paths between entity and root node of the two different sentences
8:	*{W1,W2}* $\leftarrow$ extract the words around path1 and path2
9:	$W \leftarrow$ concat(W1,W2)
10:	**Else**
11:	$W \leftarrow$ put the words around the shortest path between two entities and the root node into {W}
12:	**Return** *{W}*

Figure 3 and Fig. 4 illustrate the instances of our extraction method. In these two figures, there are two same complicated sentences. Due to the different locations of entities, they belong to different categories. It can be seen that the dependency syntactic information extracted by our strategy is generalized and distinguishable. It is easy to judge the categories of these two instances from their different syntactic information.

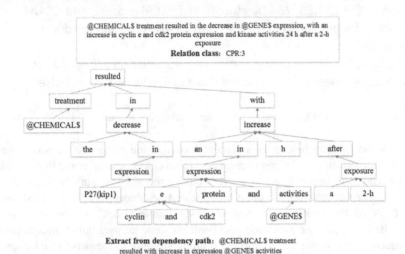

Fig. 3. Dependency syntactic parsing of category CPR:3.

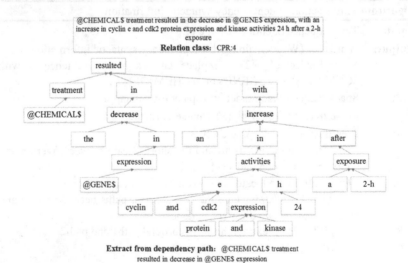

Fig. 4. Dependency syntactic parsing of category CPR:4.

2.3 BERT Representations

BERT is a contextualized word representation model, which is pre-trained based on a masked language model using multi-layer bidirectional Transformers. The input sequence of BERT is a single sentence of a group of sentences. The special token [CLS] is always the first token of every sequence, different sentences in each sequence are separated by a special token [SEP]. Since BERT has been widely used at present, this paper omits the description of the Transformer encoder and the details of BERT.

In our method, the dependency syntactic information has been extracted in the previous section. As the supplementary information, the syntactic information would be appended to the original sequence by separator [SEP]. Referring to the research of Soares et al. [13], special token [ENTITY START] and [ENTITY END] is augmented to mark the beginning and end of each entity mention, which is conducive to capture the contextual representations of entity mention. With the Transformer encoder, the contextual representations can be acquired and we mainly focus on the representations of CLS, ENTITY START, ENTITY END, and the syntactic information.

2.4 Fusion of Sequence and Syntactic Information

As for the contextual representations, the output of CLS token is H_0, the outputs of the four entity markers are H_i, H_j, H_k, and H_l respectively, the outputs of the dependency syntactic information are $\{H_x, H_{x+1}, H_{x+2},..., H_y\}$. For the target entities, representations between H_i and H_j represent the first entity, and representations between H_k and H_l represent the second entity. An average operation is applied to the entity marker representations of each entity while the CLS representation H_0 would be directly inputted into the next layer. Besides, a mean-pooling operation is also applied to the outputs of the dependency syntactic information. All of the outputs would be input into the activation + fully-connected + dropout layer. This section consists of three operations: the input vectors are firstly transformed by the Tanh activation function, then they would be fed into a fully-connected layer for feature mapping. Finally, a dropout layer is used to discard some neural network units. The whole process can be expressed as the following equation:

$$H_0^{'} = \text{dropout}(W_0(\tanh(H_0)) + b_0) \qquad (1)$$

$$H_1^{'} = \text{dropout}\left(W_1\left(\tanh\left(\frac{H_i + H_j}{2}\right)\right) + b_1\right) \qquad (2)$$

$$H_2^{'} = \text{dropout}\left(W_2\left(\tanh\left(\frac{H_k + H_l}{2}\right)\right) + b_2\right) \qquad (3)$$

$$H_3^{'} = \text{dropout}\left(W_3\left(\tanh\left(\frac{1}{y - x + 1}\sum_{t=x}^{y}H_t\right)\right) + b_3\right) \qquad (4)$$

where the weight matrix W_0, W_1, W_2, W_3 have the same dimensions, i.e. W_0, W_1, W_2, $W_3 \in R^{d \times d}$, d is the hidden state size from BERT, b_0, b_1, b_2, b_3 is the corresponding bias.

The outputs of sequence information and syntactic information are then concatenated, and the features are mapped to the category feature space through a fully-connected layer. This step can be expressed as the following equation:

$$z = W_z \left(\text{concat}\left[H_0', H_1', H_2', H_3' \right] \right) + b_z \tag{5}$$

where $W_z \in R^{4 \times d \times n}$, n is the number of relation category, d is also the hidden state size from BERT.

For classifying, a softmax layer is applied to produce the probability distribution over all relation categories, the equation is as follows:

$$p(y|x) = \text{softmax}\left(W_p * z + b \right) \tag{6}$$

where $y \in Y$, y is the target relation category, Y is the set of all relation categories, x is the current instance, $Wp \in R^{d \times |Y|}$. As the same as the previous multi-classification task, the cross-entropy function is used as the loss function for training model.

3   Experiments

3.1   CPI Extraction and Dataset

CPI extraction is generally a task of classifying whether a specified relation holds between the chemical and protein entities within a sentence or document. It can be regarded as a multi-class classification task. The ChemProt corpus is a manually annotated CPI dataset, consists of three kinds of files: abstract file, entities annotation file, and relation annotation file. A series of chemical-protein interactions can be extracted from these files. The corpus contains 10-type relation categories, as shown in Table 1. CPR:3, CPR:4, CPR:5, CPR:6, CPR:9 are the positive categories, the rest are the negative categories.

ChemProt corpus has been modified over several version and there are some differences in ChemProt used in different papers. This paper directly adopts the original

Table 1. The semantic relations in ChemProt corpus.

Relation class	Eval	ChemProt relations
CPR:1	N	Part of
CPR:2	N	Regular
CPR:3	Y	Upregulator and activator
CPR:4	Y	Downregulator and inhibitor
CPR:5	Y	Agonist
CPR:6	Y	Antagonist
CPR:7	N	Modulator
CPR:8	N	Cofactor
CPR:9	Y	Substrate and product of
CPR:10	N	Not

ChemProt corpus (version 1.0) obtained from the BioCreative VI website [19], and apply the other methods to the corpus when doing the comparative experiment.

The statistics of the ChemProt dataset are shown in Table 2. Among the 15739 sentences, there are three kinds of entities: CHEMICAL entity, GENE-Y entity, and GENE-N entity. @CHEMICAL$ is used to tag the CHEMICAL entity, @GENE$ is used to tag the GENE-Y and GENE-N entity, @CHEM-GENE$ is used to tag the overlapping entity. We adopt micro-averaged F1 as the evaluation metric. Model is evaluated by calculating the micro-averaged F1 of five positive categories (CPR:3, CPR:4, CPR:5, CPR:6, CPR:9).

Table 2. The statistics of the ChemProt dataset.

	Train	Dev	Test	Total
Abstracts	1020	612	800	2432
Sentence	6437	3558	5744	15739
Positive	4172	2427	3469	10068
Negative	2265	1131	2275	5671
CPR:3	777	552	667	1996
CPR:4	2260	1103	1667	5030
CPR:5	173	116	198	487
CPR:6	235	199	293	727
CPR:9	727	457	644	1828

3.2 Experimental Settings

In the extraction of dependency syntactic information, spacy [14] is used to obtain the parse trees of sentences. According to our method, the core dependency syntactic information is extracted from parse trees. In the model section, OpenNRE [15], an open-source PyTorch-based relation extraction framework, is used to implement our proposed model. $BERT_{PubMed-Base}$, a pre-trained on PubMed abstracts BERT model provided by Peng et al. [16], is used to initialize the weight of our model. In this paper, training set and development set are merged as a whole training set. The validation set is randomly chosen from the training samples with a 10% rate. Validation set is used to adjust the parameters, while test set is used to evaluate the performance.

All of the experiments are done on Nvidia 1080ti GPU, max length of input sequence is set as 256, batch_size is set as 8, the number of training iterations is set as 5, the optimization method is Adam, the learning rate of Adam is set as $2e - 5$, the dropout rate is set as 0.1.

3.3 In Comparison of the Other Pre-trained Model-Based Methods

Since our proposed method is an improvement of pre-trained model on CPI extraction, we abandon the comparison of some traditional methods whose performances are not satisfactory, and only compare our method with BERT model and some excellent variations of BERT. The comparison methods are listed as follows:

1) BERT model [10].
2) BERT + MTB. A method proposed by Soares et al. [13], utilizing Entity marker tokens to help relation extraction on the basis of BERT.
3) R-BERT. A model developed by Wu et al. [17], enriching pre-trained language model with entity information for relation classification.
4) BioBERT. A pre-trained biomedical language representation model developed by Lee et al. [5] for biomedical text mining. They changed the pre-trained corpus of BERT from wiki to Pubmed and PMC, which improves the performance of BERT on biomedical tasks.
5) BERT + Gaussian. A method proposed by Sun et al. [6], introducing.gaussian probability distribution and external biomedical knowledge into BERT.
6) SciBERT (replacement). A method based on SciBERT proposed by Liu et al. [18], which replace the target entities with uniform words.

For the fairness of the experiment, all of the methods use $BERT_{PubMed-Base}$ to initialize the weight as the same as our method, except for BioBERT and SciBERT using their own model. For BERT, BioBERT, and BERT + Gaussian, we directly use the source code attached in their paper for experiment. For BERT + MTB and R-BERT, they are applied to the SemEval-2010 dataset and we transfer them to the CPI dataset. We directly adopt the implementation of BERT + MTB in OpenNRE and implement R-BERT based on OpenNRE. To reduce the potential bias, all of the methods adopt the same parameters and we repeated each experiment three times to report the average F-score, precision, and recall.

Table 3. The comparison of other pre-train model and our method.

Method	P (%)	R (%)	F1 (%)
BERT	85.53	85.73	85.63
BERT + MTB	82.98	89.51	86.12
R-BERT	84.26	89.19	86.65
BioBERT	85.02	85.26	85.19
BERT + Gaussian	83.20	89.85	86.40
SciBERT (replacement)	81.40	87.90	84.50
Ours	**84.43**	**90.02**	**87.13**

The result is shown in Table 3. It can be seen that since the pre-trained models adopted in methods have spent a lot of resources on pre-training the biomedical literature, all of the methods can achieve relatively good performance. Limited by the quality of pre-trained biomedical data and the unified Transformer structure within the model, F-score of each method does not have big difference. Moreover, thanks to the pre-extracted dependency syntactic information, our pre-trained model obtains an F-score of 87.13%, which substantially outperform the state-of-the-art pre-trained model on CPI extraction. We also observe that in repeated experiments, the best F-score of other methods is difficult to exceed 87% although with the adjustment of parameters, while our proposed method can achieve 87% F-score.

We further analyze the achieving performance of our method. Compared with other methods, our proposed method can achieve the highest F-score on CPR:3, CPR:4, CPR:5, CPR:6. According to our analysis, These four kinds of CPI categories have some relatively obvious recognition words, such as the CPR:3 is corresponding to 'upregulator' and 'activator', CPR:5 is corresponding to 'agonist'. For 'upregulator', the keywords in sentence are usually 'stimulate', 'activate', 'induce', 'increase', etc. For 'agonist', the key words in sentence are usually 'agonists of', 'co-agonist', etc. Most of these keywords are verbs or prepositions, which usually have syntactic dependency relation with entities and can be captured into dependency syntactic information in our extraction method. Such as the 'resulted in decrease' in the example shown in Fig. 3. Therefore, the dependency syntactic information consisting of a series of keywords can provide some guidance for the pre-trained model, which is helpful to improve the performance.

3.4 Ablation Study

We hope to further understand the specific contributions of each component in our designed method. Thus the following ablation experiment is established.

The first configuration is to discard the pre-trained model $BERT_{PubMed-Base}$ provided by Peng et al. [16], and use the original $BERT_{Base}$ pre-trained on Wiki as an alternative. This method is labelled as Ours (no biomedical pre-trained model).

The second configuration is only using the biomedical sequence information as the input, discarding the input of dependency syntactic information. This method is labeled as Ours (no syntactic information).

The third configuration is to change the extraction method of dependency syntactic information. That is, we do not extract the words around the two shortest paths between two entities and the root node. Instead, we extract the words that are up to distance 1 away from the two shortest paths. This method is labeled as Ours (syntactic path = 1).

Table 4 reports the results of our ablation study. It is observed that the performance is decreased remarkably without the model pre-trained on the biomedical text. This demonstrates that for specified NLP tasks, pre-trained on a large amount of corresponding data plays a significant role in performance. Besides, adding too much dependency syntactic information and not adding dependency syntactic information, result in a similar decrease in performance. That means appropriately adding dependency syntactic information is conducive to improve the performance of our method on relation extraction task, while adding too much information may bring extra noise, which causes the counterproductive effect. Overall, both the good pre-trained model and the appropriate dependency syntactic information make a great contribution to the improvement of our method.

Table 4. Comparison of our methods with different components.

Method	P (%)	R (%)	F1(%)
Ours	84.43	90.02	87.13
Ours (no biomedical pre-train model)	81.65	86.93	84.21
Ours (no syntactic information)	85.52	87.71	86.58
Ours (syntactic path = 1)	84.13	89.54	86.41

4   Conclusions and Future Work

This paper develops an approach to enrich pre-trained language model with dependency syntactic information for chemical-protein interaction extraction. Our method extracts the highly generalized dependency syntactic information from CPI data, and then use BERT to generate sequence information representations and syntactic information representations. After the fusion of sequence information and syntactic information, the output would be fed into the softmax layer to obtain the final classifying result. The core syntactic information captured from the sentence improves the performance of our model. The evaluations on ChemProt corpus show that our model outperforms other pre-trained model-based methods. And the ablation study shows that a good pre-trained model and appropriate dependency syntactic information is conducive to chemical-protein interaction extraction.

In the future, we aim to utilize the syntactic information of biomedical text more effectively and further adapt our method to more biomedical datasets.

Acknowledgement. The research of this paper was supported by National Natural Science Foundation of China (61976239), Zhongshan Innovation Foundation of High-end Scientific Research Institutions (2019AG031).

References

1. Krallinger, M., Rabal, O., Akhondi, S. A.: Overview of the BioCreative VI chemical-protein interaction Track. In: Proceedings of the sixth BioCreative challenge evaluation workshop, vol. 1, pp. 141–146 (2017)
2. Lung, P.Y., Zhao, T., He, Z.: Extracting chemical protein interactions from literature. In: Proceedings of 2017 BioCreative VI Workshop, Maryland, USA, pp. 160–163 (2017)
3. Corbett, P., Boyle, J.: Improving the learning of chemical–protein interactions from literature using transfer learning and specialized word embeddings. Database, 1–10 (2018)
4. Peng, Y., Rios, A., Kavuluru, R., Lu, Z.: Extracting chemical–protein relations with ensembles of SVM and deep learning models. Database, 1–9 (2018)
5. Lee, J., et al.: BioBERT: a pre-trained biomedical language representation model for biomedical text mining. arXiv:1901.08746 (2019)
6. Sun, C., et al.: Chemical-protein interaction extraction via gaussian probability distribution and external biomedical knowledge. arXiv:1911.09487 (2019)
7. Vaswani, A., et al.: Attention is all you need. In: Advances in Neural Information Processing Systems, pp. 5998–6008 (2017)

8. Zhang, Y., Lin, H., Yang, Z., Wang, J., Sun, Y.: Chemical–protein interaction extraction via contextualized word representations and multihead attention. Database (2019)
9. Phu, M., Jason, P., Shikha, B., Samuel, R.: Do Attention Heads in BERT Track Syntactic Dependencies? arXiv:1911.12246 (2019)
10. Devlin, J., Chang, M.-W., Lee, K., Toutanova, K.: BERT: pre-training of deep bidirectional transformers for language understanding. In: Proceedings of the Conference of the North American Chapter of the Association for Computational Linguistics, pp. 4171–4186 (2019)
11. Miwa, M., Bansal, M.: End-to-end relation extraction using LSTMs on sequences and tree structures. In: Proceedings of the 54th Annual Meeting of the Association for Computational Linguistics, pp. 1105–1116. ACL, Berlin (2016)
12. Zhang, Y., Qi, P., Manning, C.D.: Graph convolution over pruned dependency trees improves relation extraction. In: Proceedings of EMNLP (2018)
13. Soares, L.B., Fitzgerald, N., Ling, J., Kwiatkowski, T.: Matching the blanks: distributional similarity for relation learning. In: Proceedings of the 57th Annual Meeting of the Association for Computational Linguistics, pp. 2895–2905. ACL, Florence (2019)
14. Spacy. https://spacy.io/. Accessed 15 Jan 2020
15. Han, X., Gao, T., Yao, Y.: OpenNRE: an open and extensible toolkit for neural relation extraction. In: Conference on Empirical Methods in Natural Language Processing & International Joint Conference on Natural Language Processing: System Demonstrations (2019)
16. Peng, Y., Yan, S., Lu, Z.: Transfer learning in biomedical natural language processing: An evaluation of BERT and ELMo on ten benchmarking datasets, In: Proceedings of the 18th BioNLP Workshop and Shared Task, vol. 1, pp. 58–65. Association for Computational Linguistics, Florence (2019)
17. Wu, S., He, Y.: Enriching pre-trained language model with entity information for relation classification. arxiv:1905.08284 (2019)
18. Liu, X., Fan, J., Dong, S.: Document-level biomedical relation extraction leveraging pre-trained self-attention structure and entity replacement. JMIR Medical Informatics (preprint) (2020)

Leveraging Label Semantics and Correlations for Judgment Prediction

Yu Fan, Lei Zhang$^{(\boxtimes)}$, and Pengfei Wang

School of Computer Science, Beijing University of Posts and Telecommunications,
Beijing, China
fanyubupt@gmail.com, {zlei,wangpengfei}@bupt.edu.cn

Abstract. Automatic judgment prediction is a classic problem in legal intelligence, which aims to predict the relevant violated articles based on the fact descriptions. Generally, both semantics and relations of articles are valuable information to solve this problem. However, previous work usually threats this problem as a classification task while these two types of information are not well explored, which makes previously proposed methods less effective. In this paper, we design a novel *G*raph-Based *La*bel *M*atching Network (GLAM for short) to address this issue. Specifically, GLAM first builds a heterogeneous graph to capture both semantics and correlations among articles. Based on this, a graph convolutional network is then utilized to learn robust article representations. Finally, a matching model is applied between article representations and fact representations to generate the matching score for judgment prediction. Experimental results on two real-world judicial datasets demonstrate that our model has more significant effect on judgement prediction than the state-of-the-art methods.

Keywords: Multi-label classification · Judgment prediction · Graph-Based Label Matching Network

1 Introduction

The task of judgment prediction aims to determine the relevant violated articles based on the fact descriptions of criminal cases. It plays an important role in legal assistant system which can provide a handy reference for legal experts and improve their working efficiency [26]. Generally, the task is regarded as a multi-label classification problem. When making predictions based on descriptions, we usually introduce articles information (e.g., semantics and relations) to improve accuracy [9,13,16]. However, consider the complexity of the judicial system, there still exists two problems that have not been completely solved or even ignored, which makes existing methods less effective, as described below:

Negligence of the Fact Relations Among Articles. Usually, the number of articles corresponding to different fact descriptions is dynamic which makes the prediction more difficult. However, previous work has not considered that

Z. Dou et al. (Eds.): CCIR 2020, LNCS 12285, pp. 70–82, 2020.
https://doi.org/10.1007/978-3-030-56725-5_6

some articles have a high probability of co-occurrence regularly based on the facts. For example, in the scenario which is similar to Table 1, intentional injury and intentional destruction of property crime have a high probability of being violated simultaneously. We define the article co-occurrence as the fact relations among articles. The fact relations which have been ignored by previous works have a great impact on judgment prediction.

Confusing Articles. There are a bunch of confusing article pairs. The definitions of them only differ in a specific act (e.g., theft and robbery) and the circumstances in corresponding cases are usually similar with each other, which lead to confusion in classification. Previous work introduced article semantic information into classification but cannot fully reveal the confusing semantic relation. Hu et al. [9] introduced several discriminative attributes but it can only solve the confusing pairs what he proposed. Others use compressed or extract label semantic information to help classify which can't fully capture the semantic relations [16,22].

Besides, previous work applied traditional deep learning models such as convolutional neural networks [11] and long short-term memory [7] to express articles, which can capture semantic and syntactic information in local consecutive word sequences well, but may ignore global word co-occurrence in a corpus which carries non-consecutive and long-distance semantics [17].

Table 1. An example of the judgment case, including a fact and two articles violated.

Fact	At 18 o'clock on August 7th, 2013, Song and Chen had a dispute, then Song held a steel pipe to beat Chen Mou, and used a steel pipe to fight the refrigerator, computer display and other property in Chen's shop...
Article	**Article 234**: Crime of intentional injury. Those who intentionally injure other people shall be sentenced to... **Article 275**: Crime of intentional destruction of properties. Deliberately destroying public and private

To solve the problems raised above, in this paper, we propose a novel *G*raph-Based *La*bel *M*atching Network (GLAM for short). We find that article relations can be more fully represented by graphs. Therefore, we introduce the graph structure for article expression.

We define articles and words in articles as nodes, and we introduce multi-relation (e.g., article-article relation, article-word relation) as edges of the graph.

Then we put the heterogeneous graph into a graph convolutional network to express article labels. Fact and label representations will be put into a matching model with co-attention mechanism to generate the affinity matrices. The final matching score is produced by aggregating affinity matrices between articles and fact for judgment.

For the purpose of evaluating the performance of our proposed model, we conduct experiments on two legal datasets. Experimental results demonstrate that our approach significantly outperforms other state-of-the-art models. We also designed several sub-experiments to verify the superiority of our structured label graph.

2   Related Work

In this section we provide a brief overview on the following three related research areas.

Judgment Prediction. Automatic judgment prediction is a typical task in legal intelligence. Generally, this task will be cast as a text classification problem. Researchers usually extract effective features from text and apply machine learning methods to make judgments [1]. Hu et al. [9] introduced discriminative attributes to enhance the connections between the fact descriptions and charges, and these attributes and charges are inferred simultaneously. Then researchers incorporate attention mechanisms for articles and facts. For example, Luo et al. [16] proposed an attention-based neural model for charge prediction by incorporating the relevant articles. Long et al. [15] utilized the attention mechanism to model the complex semantic relations among facts, pleas, and articles. Wang et al. [22] introduced unified dynamic pairwise attention model for classifications over articles. In their work, a pairwise attention model based on article definitions is incorporated into the classification model to help alleviate the case imbalance problem and confusing charge classification problem. But these methods do not consider to leverage article information adequately.

Graph Convolutional Networks. Graph Convolutional Networks (GCN) approaches fall into spectral-based and spatial-based [23]. Among them, the application of spectral-based method is more extensive currently. Henaff et al. [6] proposed a strategy to learn the graph structure from the data and applied the model to image recognition, text categorization. Bruna et al. [2] proposed the first spectral convolutional neural network on graphs. Defferrard et al. [4] optimized spectral GCN by defining a filter as Chebyshev polynomials of the diagonal matrix of eigenvalues. Kipf and Welling [12] simplified the original frameworks to improve scalability and classification performance in large-scale networks. GCN is applied to deal with structured datasets, so a number of papers viewed a document or a sentence as a graph of word nodes for text classification [2,4,6,12,17]. Yao et al. [24] regarded the documents and words as nodes and construct the corpus graph.

Semantic Matching. The semantic matching is usually applied to learn the similarity information. Generally, they create a matching matrix which is well for scenarios like question answering [14], natural language inference, and information retrieval [10], etc. Hu et al. [8] firstly generates local matching patterns and composites them by multiple convolution layers to produce the matching score. Shen et al. [20] utilized the word level similarity matrix to discover fine-grained alignment of two sentences. Guo introduced a novel retrieval model by viewing the match between queries and documents as a transportation problem [5]. Wan et al. [21] applied Bi-LSTM to sentences and introduced interaction tensor to calculate the match between sentences. This technique benefits model to learn the semantics with richer representations and then perform matching with these representations. In our work, we use labels representation from GCN and facts pair for semantic matching, by this we formalize the traditional crime classification task into a matching task.

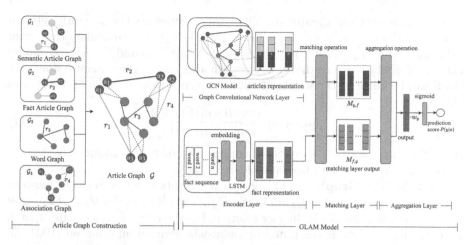

Fig. 1. On the left is the article graph construction process, on the right is the overall architecture of Graph-Based Label Matching Network (GLAM).

3   Method

In this section, we start with the problem formalization of judgement prediction. We then describe the construction of article graph $\mathcal{G}$. Based on these we introduce our GLAM model in detail. We finally present the learning and prediction procedure of GLAM.

3.1   Formalization

In judgment classification, let $X = \{x_1, x_2, \ldots, x_{|X|}\}$ denote all the facts, $\mathcal{A} = \{a_1, a_2, \ldots, a_{|A|}\}$ denote all the articles, $Y = \{y_1, y_2, \ldots, y_{|Y|}\}$ denote the set of all possible label concepts where each $y_i \in (0, 1)$ indicates whether article a_i is violated or not. $|X|$ and $|Y| = |A|$ represent the total number of facts and labels. Each instance is represented as a tuple (x_k, Y_k), where $x_k \in X$ represents the k-th fact, $Y_k \subseteq Y$ represents the article set assigned to x_k.

Given a fact x and the article set $\mathcal{A}$, we aim to generate a relevance score for each label y to check whether they are relevant or not.

3.2   Article Graph Construction

In this study, we construct an undirected heterogeneous graph $\mathcal{G} = (\mathcal{V}, \mathcal{E}, \mathcal{R})$ to formulate different information of articles where $\mathcal{V}$, $\mathcal{E}$, $\mathcal{R}$ are the set of nodes, edges and relations respectively. As Fig. 1 shows, $\mathcal{G}$ can be divided into four sub-graphs $\mathcal{G} = \mathcal{G}_1 \cup \mathcal{G}_2 \cup \mathcal{G}_3 \cup \mathcal{G}_4$, which represent four types of relations correspondingly: (1) an article graph $\mathcal{G}_1$ modeling semantic relations (2) an article graph $\mathcal{G}_2$ modeling fact relations (3) a word graph $\mathcal{G}_3$ indicating the word co-occurrence between pairs of words, and (4) an association graph $\mathcal{G}_4$ involving association relations between articles and their words.

Semantic Article Graph $\mathcal{G}_1$. This graph represents the semantic relation between articles. It is denoted as $\mathcal{G}_1 = (\mathcal{V}_1, \mathcal{E}_1, \mathcal{R}_1)$. In particular, the set of nodes $\mathcal{V}_1 = \mathcal{A} = \{a_1, a_2...a_{|A|}\}$ includes all of the articles, and $\mathcal{R}_1$ is the semantic relation. We define $s(a)$ as the set of words in article a, so the semantic similarity which can be taken as the weight of edge between article a_i and a_j is written as follows:

$$g(a_i, a_j) = \frac{count(s(a_i) \bigcap s(a_j))}{count(s(a_i) \bigcup s(a_j))} \tag{1}$$

where the numerator is the number of common words in two articles, the denominator is the number of all words in them.

Fact Article Graph $\mathcal{G}_2$. This graph represents the fact relation between articles which is denoted as $\mathcal{G}_2 = (\mathcal{V}_2, \mathcal{E}_2, \mathcal{R}_2)$. The set of nodes $\mathcal{V}_2 = \mathcal{A}$ includes all of the articles, and $\mathcal{R}_2$ is the fact relation. For the edge of article pair (a_i, a_j), the correlation weight is computed by point-wise mutual information (PMI) [3] as follows:

$$\text{PMI}(a_i, a_j) = log \frac{p(a_i, a_j)}{p(a_i) \times p(a_j)} \tag{2}$$

where $p(a_i, a_j)$ is the probability of article a_i and a_j are violated in one fact which is calculated by dividing the number of occurrences by the total number, and $p(a_i)$ is the probability of article a_i is violated in one fact. Considering that our graph has no negative weights, this edge will not exist when the $PMI(a_i, a_j)$ is less than 0.

Word Graph $\mathcal{G}_3$. This graph represents the word co-occurrence relation between words which is denoted as $\mathcal{G}_3 = (\mathcal{V}_3, \mathcal{E}_3, \mathcal{R}_3)$. The set of nodes $\mathcal{V}_3 = W$ which represents all of the words in articles. The edges between words are built by word co-occurrence in the whole corpus. We still choose PMI measure to calculate the weight between two words.

Association Graph $\mathcal{G}_4$. This graph formulates the connection among the articles and their words, we define it as $\mathcal{G}_4 = (\mathcal{V}_4, \mathcal{E}_4, \mathcal{R}_4)$. The set of nodes $\mathcal{V}_4 = \{A \bigcup W\}$. The edge between the tuple of article and word are built by word occurrence in articles. The weight of edge is term frequency-inverse document frequency (TF-IDF) of the word in the article. Obviously, applying TF-IDF as weight is better than applying term frequency because TF-IDF tends to give high weights for words that are important to this article, and low weights for words that are common to all articles.

3.3   GLAM Model

This section describes our Graph-Based Label Matching Network (GLAM) in detail. Figure 1 shows the architecture of GLAM model.

Graph Convolutional Network Layer. From the above, we build a heterogeneous graph $\mathcal{G}$ with the correlation matrix A where each element is calculated in the method defined above. The weight of edge will be zero when there is no edge between two nodes. Besides, we define a feature matrix X containing semantic features about words and articles. Then we apply a GCN model to generate new article representations. Considering efficiency and effectiveness, we take a 2-layer GCN with randomly initialized weights:

$$Z = \hat{A} \, ReLU(\hat{A}XW^{(0)})W^{(1)} \tag{3}$$

where $Z \in R^{n \times k}$ is the output matrix, W^0 and W^1 are parameters need to learn, and k is the dimension of output features. And $\hat{A} = D^{-\frac{1}{2}}AD^{-\frac{1}{2}}$ where D is the degree matrix of graph G. As Fig. 1 shows, two types of article nodes output two types of representations. We concatenate two types of representations as the final article representations which can be formulated as $V_Y \in R^{|Y| \times 2k}$.

Encoder Layer. In this section, we will design a encoder to generate fact representations. In juridical field, each fact is described by a set of words. The encoder encodes the discrete input sequence into continuous hidden states. More formally, we define $\mathbf{V} = \{\mathbf{v}_i \in \mathbb{R}^d | i = 1, 2, \dots\}$ denote all the word vectors for each fact in a D-dimensional continuous space. Given each fact x, we aggregate the word vectors to obtain its semantic matrix $\mathbf{V}_f$ as $[\mathbf{h}_f(1), ..., \mathbf{h}_f(n)]$, where n is the fixed length of $\mathbf{V}_f$, and $\mathbf{h}_f(t)$ are regarded as the representation at time step t, which are obtained by LSTM [7]:

$$\mathbf{h}_f(t) = LSTM(\mathbf{v}_t : t \in x, \mathbf{v}_t \in \mathbf{V}, \mathbf{h}_f(t-1)) \tag{4}$$

Matching Layer. Matching layer is dedicated to select attentive semantics from both facts and labels to generate relevance scores for matching. We have contextual vector representations of the context $V_f \in R^{n \times h}$ as fact representations from encoder layer. And we get the expression of labels (i.e., articles) $V_Y \in R^{|Y| \times 2k}$ where $h = 2k$ from GCN layer. Then we propose a co-attention mechanism to compute the affinity matrix between facts and labels:

$$\begin{aligned} M_{f,y} &= s(V_Y V_f^T)V_f \\ M_{y,f} &= s((V_Y V_f^T)^T)V_Y \end{aligned} \tag{5}$$

where $s(\cdot)$ is the softmax function to the second dimension. $M_{f,y}$ and $M_{y,f}$ are fact-to-articles and articles-to-fact affinity matrices respectively.

Aggregation Layer. In aggregation layer, we will integrate attention context between articles and fact to obtain the matching score. We employ the sigmoid function $\sigma(\cdot)$ to output the relevance score of (x, y) through Eq. (6)

$$P(y|x) = \sigma(\mathbf{w}_y \cdot [g(\mathbf{M}_{f,y}); g(\mathbf{M}_{y,f})]) \tag{6}$$

where $\mathbf{w}_y$ is parameter need to learn, and $g(\cdot)$ aggregates one matrix by columns into a single vector.

3.4   Learning and Prediction

Finally, by considering all facts and their label sets, we obtain our learning approach as follows:

$$\mathcal{L}(x, Y_x) = \sum_{x \in X} \left(\sum_{y \in Y_x} \left(\ln P(y, x) - \sum_{\bar{y} \in C - Y_x} \ln P(\bar{y}, x) \right) \right) \tag{7}$$

where $\bar{y}$ is each negative label mined from siblings of y. We use the Adam optimizer and update the parameters of our model for each iteration according to Eq.(7).

To summarize, the matching strategy can be described as: for all article labels, we first generate their representations through GCN model. Based on the fixed label representations, given a fact x, the best label set is a combination of assignments with the highest score from each label given the input:

$$O_y(x,y) = \sum_{y \in C} I(P(y,x) > \delta_y) \qquad (8)$$

where $I(\cdot)$ denotes the indicator function, $O_y(x,y)$ is the relevance score function when feeding label set y to x, and δ_y is the learned threshold of label y.

According to Eq. (6) and Eq. (7), for each fact, we only need to conduct a forward computation to generate the scores for each label.

Table 2. Statistics of the two legal datasets for experiments.

Dataset	#Fact	#Articles	Average fact description size	Average article definition size	Average law set size per fact	Average article set size per fact
Fraud	17,160	70	1,455	136	2.6	4.3
CAIL	204,231	183	1,444	129	1.4	1.3

4 Experiment

In this section, we evaluate GLAM by comparing with several state-of-the-art methods. We first introduce the experimental settings, then we analyze the experimental results on the judgment prediction task.

4.1 Dataset and Experimental Setup

This section describes the dataset and experimental settings of our work.

Dataset. We ran our experiments on two real-world legal datasets which are Fraud dataset and CAIL dataset respectively.

- **Fraud** [22] comprises 17,160 criminal cases related with fraud. These data are crawled from China Judgment Online[1] and span from Jan. 2016 to June. 2016.

---

[1] http://wenshu.court.gov.cn/.

- **CAIL**[26] a public dataset from Chinese AI and Law challenge (CAIL2018). The cases in the dataset contain two parts, i.e., fact description and corresponding judgment result (including laws, articles, and charges).

We extract fact descriptions and applicable articles from datasets. After preprocessing we obtain $17,160$ facts on the Fraud dataset, and $204,231$ facts on the CAIL dataset. The detailed statistics of two datasets are shown in are shown in Table 2. Finally, we split all the datasets into two non-overlapping parts, the training set and testing set, with a ratio 8:2 and we randomly selected 10% of training set as validation set.

Parameter Settings. For the baselines, to make a fair comparison, we follow the reported optimal parameter settings and optimize them using the validation set. We implement our method in Pytorch. In GCN layer, we use 300-dimensional GloVe [18] word embeddings as the word feature. We set the batch size as 64, embedding dim of fact encoder as 300, the dimension of output feature in GCN as 128, and the hidden size of encoder layer as 256. We use Adam optimizer which is determined from 0.1 to 0.0001. The initial learning rate is 0.0015 with 0.9 exponential decay. For each fact description, we set maximum number of words is 500.

Evaluation Metric. We adopt Jaccard, macro precision (Macro-P), macro recall (Macro-R) and macro F-measure (Macro-F) which are widely used in the classification task to evaluate the performance. Differences are considered statistically significant when the p–value is lower than 0.05.

4.2 Baselines

To evaluate the performance of our methods, we compare our model[2] with the following methods:

- **BP-MLL**: It is derived from the popular backpropagation algorithm that captures the characteristics of multi-label learning by replacing its error function with a defined new error function [25].
- **CC**: Classifier Chains [19] is a binary association method for multi-label classification, thinking that each label is an independent binary problem.
- **TextCNN-MLL**: A convolutional neural network [11] which denotes multiple filter widths as text classifier, and employs a new error function similar to BP-MLL.
- **TOPJUDGE**: A topological multi-task learning framework for judgment prediction [26], which applies multiple subtasks and DAG dependencies to judgment prediction.
- **DPAM**: A unified Dynamic Pairwise Attention Model [22] that fusing article semantics into a pairwise attention matrix for judgment prediction. We use sequential form of DAG to model the dependencies between laws and articles.

CC and TextCNN-MLL were using Scikit–multilearn. For DPAM, BP-MLL, and TOPJUDGE, we use the code released by their authors.

---

[2] https://github.com/IntelligentLaw/GLAM.

Table 3. Performance on judgment prediction between the baselines and GLAM (all the values in the table are percentage numbers with% omitted). The best performance in each case is written in bold.

Dataset	Fraud				CAIL			
Metrics	Macro-P	Macro-R	Macro-F	Jaccard	Macro-P	Macro-R	Macro-F	Jaccard
BP-MLL	45.1	30.4	34.4	60.1	41.6	30.2	33.6	59.7
CC	43.2	28.6	33.6	58.5	42.1	32.5	35.6	62.6
TextCNN-MLL	68.5	34.3	40.5	65.5	76.3	54.3	60.1	72.3
TOPJUDGE	68.9	35.1	40.7	65.8	77.1	54.9	61.1	72.9
DPAM	71.2	35.5	43.5	67.9	78.3	57.7	63.3	74.9
GLAM	**71.5**	**46.5**	**52.8**	**75.2**	**81.1**	**68.1**	**71.5**	**81.5**

4.3 Comparison Against Baselines

We compare GLAM to the state-of-the-art baseline methods for judgment prediction. The experimental results on the two datasets are shown in Table 3. The results show obviously that our model achieves the best performance on all metrics.

Compared with DPAM which performs best among baselines, we can infer that our model has highly improved on Macro-R (10.4% in CAIL and 10.0% in Fraud) and slightly improved in Macro-P (2.8% in CAIL and 0.3% in Fraud). This phenomenon might indicates that for each fact, the accuracy of predicting its positive label sets (violated articles) has been greatly improved, and the probability of misjudging irrelevant articles decreases slightly. DPAM considers semantic interactions between each pair of articles which does not adequately leverages information of articles. That is the reason why GLAM performs better than DPAM.

In other methods of baselines, the shallow model BP-MLL and CC performs worst. Comparing two models, CC performs well on Fraud dataset but not as good as BP-MLL on another dataset. The reason is that CC mechanism is flawed: if CC misclassifies a label, the incorrect label is passed on to the next classifier and sway the next classifier to a wrong decision [19]. The other three deep neural models in baselines performs better than shallow model. The result of TextCNN-MLL represents the ability of deep neural networks to learn representations more powerfully than shallow model. TOPJUDGE take the topological properties of multi-task into consideration but have a lower performance than DPAM. The reason is that both models use a multitasking learning framework, but DPAM introduces a pairwise attention mechanism based on article definitions to alleviate the label imbalance problem. In conclusion, GLAM achieves promising improvements which indicates the effectiveness of our model.

4.4 Analysis on the Graph of Articles

GLAM design a graph containing semantics and multi-relation among articles (e.g., semantic relations and fact relations). Then we put the heterogeneous

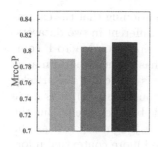 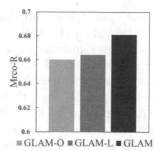 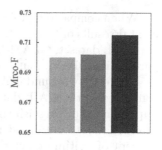

■ GLAM-O ■ GLAM-L ■ GLAM

Fig. 2. Performance comparison of the GLAM model with its two sub-variant models GLAM-O and GLAM-L on CAIL dataset in terms of Marco-P, Macro-R and Macro-F1.

Table 4. Performance on judgment prediction between GLAM and GLAM-L (all the values in the table are percentage numbers with% omitted)

Dataset	Fraud				CAIL			
Metrics	Macro-P	Macro-R	Macro-F	Jaccard	Macro-P	Macro-R	Macro-F	Jaccard
GLAM-L	70.7	44.5	50.9	74.7	80.5	66.4	70.2	81.0
GLAM	**71.5**	**46.5**	**52.8**	**75.2**	**81.1**	**68.1**	**71.5**	**81.5**

graph into a graph convolutional network. In this section we conducted experiments to verify that the various article information we introduced has worked.

Firstly, we delete the edges that represent fact relations among articles from our model and name it GLAM-L. The performance comparison between GLAM and GLAM-L is shown in Table 4. We can observe that GLAM gets the greatest improvement in Macro-R (2.0% in Fraud and 1.7% in CAIL). This proves that introducing fact relations in articles can increase the proportion of positive cases predictions. The performance improvement of GLAM on Macro-P metric is slight (0.8% and 0.6%), it indicates that the factual relation is less effective when predicting irrelevant articles. Correspondingly, when judging irrelevant articles, semantic information (other parts of the graph) have a greater effect.

Then, we delete all edges between articles which means remove the article relations from GLAM. We get a model that only contains word occurrence in articles and word co-occurrence information [24], which is named GLAM-O. We further compare the two sub-models GLAM-O and GLAM-L as well as GLAM to show their different effectiveness. From the result which shows in Fig. 2 we have the following observation: (1) A graph containing only word co-occurrence information and word occurrence in articles information can give a relatively good result, but not as good as the other two. (2) Adding semantic relations between articles on the basis of GLAM-O has slightly improved the performance, we can regard it as a supplement to the semantic information. (3) GLAM performs best on all metrics which verifies the significance of considering both semantics and two types of label relations for judgment prediction.

When comparing Table 3 and Table 4, it is worth mentioning that the experimental results of GLAM-L and DPAM on Macro-P are different in two datasets. On CAIL dataset, GLAM-L achieve a significant improvement on Macro-P compared with DPAM. But on Fraud dataset, GLAM-L has reduced performance on Macro-P by around 0.5% compared with DPAM. This is because the articles contained in the CAIL dataset are parallel (e.g., theft and robbery), it is more important to distinguish the differences of the keywords between them. But the Fraud dataset contains definitions of many concepts in judgment such as the concept of legitimate defense and joint crime which need more contextual information for classification. However, the application of the label relations in facts can effectively make up for this deficiency.

5   Conclusion

Judgment prediction is a crucial task in legal intelligence which leverages label information inadequately. We emphasize the importance of label semantics and relations, then we define label correlations and introduce the graph neural network to construct the label information. Moreover, we encode facts and put facts and labels representations into a matching model with co-attention mechanism to generate a relevance score for judgment. The experimental results show that GLAM achieves outperforms baseline methods and the information we introduced improves the judgment prediction.

In the future, we will explore from the following two aspects: (1) we will further analyze the significance of articles information to judgment prediction. (2) we will apply our model to other complex multi-task text classification problems.

Acknowledgments. This research work was partially supported by the National Natural Science Foundation of China under Grant No. 61802029, and Open Project Funding of CAS-NDST Lab under Grant No. CASNDST202005.

References

1. Aletras, N., Tsarapatsanis, D., Preoţiucpietro, D., Lampos, V.: Predicting judicial decisions of the european court of human rights: a natural language processing perspective. Peer J **2** (2016)
2. Bruna, J., Zaremba, W., Szlam, A., Lecun, Y.: Spectral networks and locally connected networks on graphs. In: International Conference on Learning Representations (ICLR) (2013)
3. Church, K.W., Hanks, P.: Word association norms, mutual information, and lexicography. Comput. Linguist. **16**(1), 22–29 (1990)
4. Defferrard, M., Bresson, X., Vandergheynst, P.: Convolutional neural networks on graphs with fast localized spectral filtering. In: Neural Information Processing Systems, pp. 3844–3852 (2016)

5. Guo, J., Fan, Y., Ai, Q., Croft, W.B.: Semantic matching by non-linear word transportation for information retrieval. In: Proceedings of the 25th ACM International on Conference on Information and Knowledge Management, pp. 701–710 (2016)
6. Henaff, M., Bruna, J., Lecun, Y.: Deep convolutional networks on graph-structured data (2015)
7. Hochreiter, S., Schmidhuber, J.: Long short-term memory. Neural Comput. **9**(8), 1735–1780 (1997)
8. Hu, B., Lu, Z., Li, H., Chen, Q.: Convolutional neural network architectures for matching natural language sentences. In: Neural Information Processing Systems (NIPS), pp. 2042–2050 (2014)
9. Hu, Z., Li, X., Tu, C., Liu, Z., Sun, M.: Few-shot charge prediction with discriminative legal attributes. In: Proceedings of the 27th International Conference on Computational Linguistics, COLING 2018, Santa Fe, New Mexico, USA, 20–26 August 2018 (2018)
10. Huang, P., He, X., Gao, J., Deng, L., Acero, A., Heck, L.P.: Learning deep structured semantic models for web search using clickthrough data, pp. 2333–2338 (2013)
11. Kim, Y.: Convolutional neural networks for sentence classification. In: Empirical Methods in Natural Language Processing, pp. 1746–1751 (2014)
12. Kipf, T.N., Welling, M.: Semi-supervised classification with graph convolutional networks. In: International Conference on Learning Representations (ICLR) (2016)
13. Lauderdale, B.E., Clark, T.S.: The supreme court's many median justices. Am. Polit. Sci. Rev. **106**(04), 847–866 (2012)
14. Lin, J.J.: An exploration of the principles underlying redundancy-based factoid question answering. ACM Trans. Inf. Syst. **25**(2), 6 (2007)
15. Long, S., Tu, C., Liu, Z., Sun, M.: Automatic judgment prediction via legal reading comprehension. CoRR abs/1809.06537 (2018)
16. Luo, B., Feng, Y., Xu, J., Zhang, X., Zhao, D.: Learning to predict charges for criminal cases with legal basis. CoRR abs/1707.09168 (2017)
17. Peng, H., et al.: Large-scale hierarchical text classification with recursively regularized deep graph-CNN. In: The Web Conference, pp. 1063–1072 (2018)
18. Pennington, J., Socher, R., Manning, C.D.: Glove: global vectors for word representation. In: EMNLP, pp. 1532–1543 (2014)
19. Read, J., Pfahringer, B., Holmes, G., Frank, E.: Classifier chains for multi-label classification. Mach. Learn. **85**(3), 333–359 (2011)
20. Shen, G., Yang, Y., Deng, Z.: Inter-weighted alignment network for sentence pair modeling. In: Proceedings of the 2017 Conference on Empirical Methods in Natural Language Processing, EMNLP 2017, Copenhagen, Denmark, 9–11 September 2017, pp. 1179–1189 (2017)
21. Wan, S., Lan, Y., Guo, J., Xu, J., Pang, L., Cheng, X.: A deep architecture for semantic matching with multiple positional sentence representations. In: National Conference on Artificial Intelligence (AAAI), pp. 2835–2841 (2016)
22. Wang, P., Yang, Z., Niu, S., Zhang, Y., Zhang, L., Niu, S.: Modeling dynamic pairwise attention for crime classification over legal articles. In: The 41st International ACM SIGIR Conference on Research & Development in Information Retrieval, pp. 485–494 (2018)
23. Wu, Z., Pan, S., Chen, F., Long, G., Zhang, C., Yu, P.S.: A comprehensive survey on graph neural networks. arXiv:Learning (2019)
24. Yao, L., Mao, C., Luo, Y.: Graph convolutional networks for text classification. In: National Conference on Artificial Intelligence (2019)

25. Zhang, M., Zhou, Z.: Multilabel neural networks with applications to functional genomics and text categorization. IEEE Trans. Knowl. Data Eng. **18**(10), 1338–1351 (2006)
26. Zhong, H., Zhipeng, G., Tu, C., Xiao, C., Liu, Z., Sun, M.: Legal judgment prediction via topological learning. In: Proceedings of the 2018 Conference on Empirical Methods in Natural Language Processing, pp. 3540–3549 (2018)

Position-aware Hybrid Attention Network for Aspect-Level Sentiment Analysis

Yongqiang Zheng[1], Xia Li[1,2(✉)], Guixin Su[1], Junteng Ma[1], and Chaolin Ning[1]

[1] School of Information Science and Technology, Guangdong University of Foreign Studies, Guangzhou, China
zhengyongqiang314@126.com, guixinsu@126.com, juntengma@126.com, chaolinning@126.com
[2] Guangzhou Key Laboratory of Multilingual Intelligent Processing, Guangzhou, China
xiali@gdufs.edu.cn

Abstract. Aspect-level sentiment analysis aims to predict the sentiment polarity of a given target in a review sentence. Most of the previous methods focus on capturing the context information of words across the sentence related to the target, ignoring the importance of the independent relationship between the opinion words and the target. To address this limitation, we propose a position-aware hybrid attention network model for aspect-level sentiment analysis, which incorporates not only the context information of words related to the target, but also the independent relationship between the opinion words related to the target. We conduct several comparable experiments on public laptop and restaurant datasets. The experimental results show that our proposed model achieves a more effective performance than the baseline models.

Keywords: Aspect-level sentiment analysis · Hybrid attention network · Context attention network · Opinion attention network

1 Introduction

Aspect-level sentiment analysis is a fine-grained task in sentiment analysis, which aims to predict sentiment polarity (i.e., positive, neutral, or negative) of a specific target of a given sentence. Aspect-level sentiment analysis can be used in many fields such as product review analysis, public opinion analysis, and stock opinion analysis etc.

A core challenge of aspect-level fine-grained sentiment analysis is to correctly find the corresponding sentiment polarity of a given aspect in a sentence which contains more than one aspect with different polarities. For example, given a sentence "*Service was slow, but the people were friendly*.", "*service*" and "*people*" are two targets of the sentence and each of them related to different opinion words "*slow*" and "*friendly*". It means that as for the "service" target, the polarity of sentiment is negative, and as for the "people" target, the polarity of sentiment is positive. Therefore, finding the relationship between the target and corresponding opinion words is important for getting the final sentiment of a target in the sentence.

Z. Dou et al. (Eds.): CCIR 2020, LNCS 12285, pp. 83–95, 2020.
https://doi.org/10.1007/978-3-030-56725-5_7

In the previous studies, various solutions are proposed to capture the context information of the given target. One solution is to use the position of opinion words in the sentence to obtain more precise relationship between opinion words and the target. For example, Zeng et al. [1] introduced the position information of words to help capture the relationship between opinion words and the target. Another solution is to model context information (not limited to the opinion words) related to the target in the sentence. For example, Tang et al. [2] used two LSTM networks to model left context information and right context information related to the target, respectively. Wang et al. [3] combined each word hidden state with aspect embedding as context information supplementation to the target. These methods achieve good performance in the task of aspect-level sentiment analysis task based on context information related to the target words in the sentence or the word location information.

However, we find that the context information captured by the above models is those words across the sentence (e.g., left context and right context). We argue that the opinion words are more important in supervising the polarity of the sentence for the given target, that is to say, we can independently consider the importance of the relationship between the target and opinion words.

To this end, we proposed a position-aware hybrid attention network based model which consists of two components, namely opinion attention network and context attention network. The context attention network is used to capture context information between words across sentence with the target, and the opinion attention network is used to incorporate independent relationship between opinion words and the target. The proposed model shows a stable improvement results in laptop and restaurant data sets. Based on our work, the main contributions are as follows:

(1) We propose a hybrid attention network to capture the context information between the words across sentence with the target, as well as the independent relationship between the opinion words and the target to obtain more precisely sentiment information of the given target in the sentence.
(2) We conduct several experiments and ablation tests on public laptop and restaurant datasets to validate our model. We will show that our model achieves a stable and effective performance compared with the baseline models.

2   Related Work

Aspect-level sentiment analysis aims to detect polarity of a sentence for a given target in a sentence. Many of the previous studies rely on rich features, such as sentiment lexicons, linguistic features and syntax etc., to help detect the sentiment. Kiritchenko et al. [4] built two sentiment lexicons for restaurant and laptop domain, and achieved good results in detecting aspects and sentiment by using these lexicons. Wagner et al. [5] combined four sentiment lexicons to design some rule-based features and extracted Bag-of-N-gram features to train a classifier for aspect-level sentiment analysis. Vo et al. [6] split a tweet into a left context and a right context according to a given target, using distributed word representations and neural pooling functions to extract features.

In recent years, different models based on neural networks are proposed and achieve good results in aspect-level sentiment analysis task due to their strong capacity to automatically extract high-level features of sentences [7–20].

As the context information of a given target is useful for improving the performance of aspect-level sentiment analysis task, some of previous studies focused on modeling context information related to the target. For example, Tang et al. [2] used two LSTM networks to model left context information and right context information related to the target words, respectively. The left and right target-dependent representations are concatenated together as the final representation of the sentence to predict the sentiment polarity of the aspect. Wang et al. [3] combined hidden states of each word with aspect embedding as context information supplementation to supervise the generation of attention vectors, and used the attention vectors to generate the final representation of the sentence. Tang et al. [7] captured the correlation between each context word and the aspect through multiple attentions and used the output of the last attention as the final representation of the sentence. Different from the above models, Ma et al. [8] used two independent LSTM networks to model aspects and contexts respectively, and used the attentive representation of aspect for the context, the concatenation of the hidden states of the two LSTM networks as the final representation of the sentence. Chen et al. [9] proposed a multi-layer architecture, in which each layer includes attention-based word feature aggregation and a GRU unit is proposed to learn the sentence representation.

Some of recent studies paid more attentions to word location information and achieved a new good results [1, 21, 22]. Zeng et al. [1] used Gaussian kernel to model the position of words. By introducing the position information into the model, their methods improved the results of the aspect-level sentiment analysis task. Wang et al. [21] introduced the ideas of global attention scores and grammar-based local attention scores for the task, a gating mechanism was used to synthesize global information and local information to generate the final representation of the sentence.

In this paper, we also focus on capturing the context information related to the given target of the sentence. We propose a hybrid attention network based model to incorporate independent relationship between opinion words and target, as well as the context information between the words across sentence with the target.

3 The Proposed Model

In this paper, a position-aware hybrid attention network is proposed for the aspect-level sentiment analysis. As shown in Fig. 1, our model mainly includes four parts: embedding layer, encoder layer, attention layer, and output layer, where the hybrid attention layer is divided into opinion attention module and context attention module.

For the context attention module, as previous work, we use aspect representation to help calculate the attention of each word across the sentence related to the target. For the opinion attention module, we use the aspect representation to help calculate the attention score of the candidate opinion words, and generate the opinion feature representation with different weights. We input the context information representation getting from the whole sentence and the opinion relationship representation getting from only the independent opinion words into a fully connected layer to get the final representation of the sentence. In our model, similar to previous work, we also introduced position embedding to be concatenated with word embedding to better obtain the position information of the words related to the target.

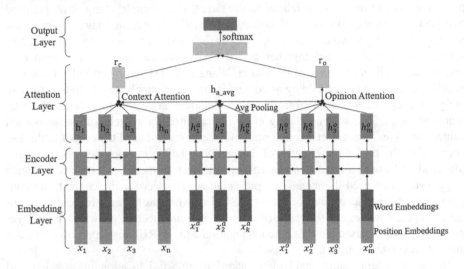

Fig. 1. The whole architecture of our model.

In the following sections, we will describe our model in more detail. Section 3.1 gives the problem definition, Sect. 3.2 introduces word position embedding, Sect. 3.3 introduces the encoding layer for sentence, target and opinion words, Sect. 3.4 introduces the hybrid attention networks and Sect. 3.5 describes the loss function of our model.

3.1 Problem Definition

Given a sentence with n number of word sequences $S = \{w_1, w_2, w_3, \ldots, w_n\}$, a target with k number of word sequences $A = \{w_1^a, w_2^a, w_3^a, \ldots, w_k^a\}$, where A is a subset of S. The purpose of aspect-level sentiment analysis is to find out the sentiment of the given target A in a context sentence S.

As said in the above section, we argue that the opinion words are also important in supervising the polarity of the sentence for the given target. In our model, we use sentiment lexicon[1] of Bin Liu [23] to extract the opinion words of the sentence. Given the sentence S, we can also get opinion words $O = \{w_1^o, w_2^o, w_3^o, \ldots, w_m^o\}$, where O is a subset of S. Then the final definition of our model is described as finding out the sentiment of the given target A in a context sentence S with extracted opinion words O.

---

[1] http://sentiment.christopherpotts.net/lexicons.html.

3.2 Word Position Embedding

Let $E \in \mathbb{R}^{d_e \times |V|}$ be the pre-trained word embedding matrix generated by the unsupervised method [24, 25], $P \in \mathbb{R}^{d_p \times |N|}$ be the position embedding matrix. Where d_e is the dimension of word embedding, $|V|$ is the vocabulary, d_p is the dimension of position embedding, and $|N|$ is the number of possible relevant positions between each word and aspect.

We define the relative distance between each word and the target as the relative offset of the word across the sentence to the target. We calculate the distance using the formula (1). Where i is the index of the each word across the sentence, j is the index of the first word in the target, k is the length of the target, and n is the length of the whole sentence.

$$
\begin{cases}
i-j & i<j \\
i-j-k & j+k<i\leq n \\
0 & j\leq i\leq j+k
\end{cases}
\tag{1}
$$

In the pre-training word embedding matrix, find each word in sentence S, opinion word O, and target A, we map them into d_e vectors. In the position embedding matrix, find each sentence in word S, opinion word O, we map them into d_p vectors. Finally, the word embedding and position embedding are concatenated together. In target A, there is no position embedding, and no concatenating is needed:

$$
x_i = [E(w_i); P(w_i)]
\tag{2}
$$

$$
x_i^o = [E(w_i^o); P(w_i^o)]
\tag{3}
$$

$$
x_i^a = E(w_i^a)
\tag{4}
$$

Where w_i, w_i^o, w_i^a represent word sequences S, opinion word O, aspect A respectively. E (w) means search in word embedding matrix, P (w) means search in position embedding matrix, [;] represents vector stitching.

3.3 Sentence, Target and Opinion Words Encoding

In our model, we use three bidirectional long short term memory (Bi-LSTM) networks [26] to encode contextual information, opinion information and aspect information respectively. For forward LSTM, we fed word embedding x_i and the hidden state at last time step $\vec{h}_{t-1}$ and the hidden state $\vec{h}_t$ can be calculated as:

$$
\vec{h}_i = \overrightarrow{LSTM}(x_i, \vec{h}_{i-1})
\tag{5}
$$

Backward LSTM does the same thing as forward LSTM except that the input sequence is fed in a reversed way. Then the hidden state of forward LSTM and

backward LSTM are concatenated and hyperbolic tangent activation function is applied
to the concatenation result to form the hidden state h_i:

$$\overleftarrow{h}_i = \overleftarrow{LSTM}(x_i, \overleftarrow{h}_{i-1}) \tag{6}$$

$$h_i = \tanh\left(\left[\overrightarrow{h}_i; \overleftarrow{h}_i\right]\right) \tag{7}$$

where $\overrightarrow{h}_i$ and $\overleftarrow{h}_i$ are the hidden state of forward LSTM and backward LSTM at time step
i respectively. The output of the Encoder layer are denoted as $H = \{h_1, h_2, h_3, h_n\}$,
$H_o = \{h_1^o, h_2^o, h_3^o, h_m^o\}$, $H_a = \{h_1^a, h_2^a, h_3^a, h_m^a\}$.

3.4   Hybrid Attention Network

As shown in Fig. 1, we design two attention modules, Opinion Attention and Context
Attention, to incorporate independent relationship information of opinion words related
to the target and context information of words related to the target across sentence. In
the two modules, Opinion Attention aims to generate precisely opinion representation
by learning the relationship between opinion words and the target, and Context
Attention makes the model focus on the words across sentence related to the target.

Opinion Attention. Opinion Attention is designed to get the independent relationship
of different opinion words and the target. As shown in Fig. 2, our opinion words
extraction strategy is as follow: we first combine the positive and negative sentiment
lexicons as a whole sentiment lexicon. Based on the combined lexicon, given a sentence S, we can get the candidate opinion words O. In order to determine the corresponding opinion words of each aspect, we also use dependency syntax analysis. The
words that are dependent on the aspect are called "direct reach", and the distance
between these words and the aspect is 1. We test different candidate opinion words
extraction strategies with different distance and the results will be discussed later.

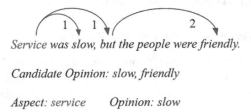

Service was slow, but the people were friendly.

Candidate Opinion: slow, friendly

Aspect: service   Opinion: slow

Fig. 2. Our opinion words extraction strategy based on dependency tree.

Given the target $H_a = \{h_1^a, h_2^a, \ldots, h_k^a\}$, and the hidden state of opinion words
$H_o = \{h_1^o, h_2^o, \ldots, h_o^o\}$, the Opinion Attention score α can be calculated by the following formulas (8–10). First, we get the average pooling of target representation

h_{a_avg}. We use the aspect representation to learn the attention score of each word across sentence related to the target α_i, where $W_{att1} \in \mathbb{R}^{2d_l}$ is the weight matrix.

$$h_{a\_avg} = \frac{1}{k} \sum_{i=1}^{k} h_i^a \qquad (8)$$

$$f_o\left(h_i^o, h_{a\_avg}\right) = h_i^o W_{att1} h_{a\_avg}^{\mathrm{T}} \qquad (9)$$

$$\alpha_i = \frac{\exp\left(f_o\left(h_i^o, h_{a\_avg}\right)\right)}{\sum_{j=1}^{n} \exp\left(f_o\left(h_j^o, h_{a\_avg}\right)\right)} \qquad (10)$$

Then, the relationship representation $r_o \in \mathbb{R}^{2d_l}$ is expressed as a weighted sum of the hidden state h_i^o and its attention score α_i as shown in formula (11):

$$r_o = \sum_{i=1}^{n} h_i^o \alpha_i \qquad (11)$$

Context Attention. Given the target representation and the hidden state of each words across sentence $H = \{h_1, h_2, \ldots, h_n\}$, the contextual attention score β can be calculated by the following formula (12–13), where, $W_{att2} \in \mathbb{R}^{2d_l}$ is the weight matrix.

$$f_c\left(h_i, h_{a\_avg}\right) = h_i W_{att2} h_{a\_avg}^{\mathrm{T}} \qquad (12)$$

$$\beta_i = \frac{\exp\left(f_c\left(h_i, h_{a\_avg}\right)\right)}{\sum_{j=1}^{n} \exp\left(f_c\left(h_j, h_{a\_avg}\right)\right)} \qquad (13)$$

Then, the context information $r_c \in \mathbb{R}^{2d_l}$ is expressed as a weighted sum of the hidden state h_i and its attention score β_i as shown in formula (14).

$$r_c = \sum_{i=1}^{n} h_i \beta_i \qquad (14)$$

From the above attention model, the relationship representation r_o and the context information r_c are obtained. Then we use a non-linear layer to project a particular aspect of the attention representation r into the class C target space, as shown in formula (15).

$$r = \tanh(W_o r_o + W_c r_c) \qquad (15)$$

Where, $W_o \in \mathbb{R}^{2d_l \times C}$ and $W_c \in \mathbb{R}^{2d_l \times C}$ are weight matrices, and C is the number of emotional polarities. Then we use softmax to calculate the sentiment distribution of r as formula (16).

$$y_i = \frac{\exp(r_i)}{\sum_{i=1}^{C} \exp(r_i)} \qquad (16)$$

3.5   Loss Function

Let $\hat{y}$ be the estimated probability distribution and y be the true distribution. We use cross entropy and L2 regularization for the parameters as the loss function, as shown in formula (17). Where i is the index of sentence, j is the index of class. N is the number of training samples, C is the number of sentiment classes, λ is the L2-regularization term. Θ is the parameter set.

$$J = -\frac{1}{N} \sum_{i=1}^{N} \sum_{j=1}^{C} y_i^j \log\left(\widehat{y_i^j}\right) + \lambda \left(\sum_{\theta \in \Theta} \theta^2 \right) \qquad (17)$$

4   Experiments

4.1   Dataset

We conducted several experiments on the data set of SemEval 2014[2] task 4 to verify the effectiveness of our model. The SemEval 2014 dataset includes comments in two areas, which are notebooks and restaurants. These comments have three emotional polarities: positive, neutral, and negative, as shown in Table 1. In addition, followed previous work, we use the accuracy as the evaluation index of the model.

Table 1. The details of the laptop and restaurant datasets.

Dataset	Positive		Negative		Neural	
	Train	Test	Train	Test	Train	Test
Laptop	994	341	870	128	464	169
Restaurant	2164	728	807	196	637	196

4.2   Experiment Settings

In our experiment, word embeddings are all initialized using a pre-trained 300 dimensional GloVe[3] word vector [24]. All words outside the vocabulary are initialized

---

[2] http://alt.qcri.org/semeval2014/task4/.
[3] https://nlp.stanford.edu/projects/glove/.

by sampling from the uniformly distributed from (−0.1, 0.1). The position embedding of sentences and opinion words is initialized using xavier uniform distribution, and the dimension is set to 100 dimensions. The weight matrix and offset are also initialized using the xavier uniform distribution. In order to perform dependency syntax analysis, the sentences of both datasets are parsed using Stanford CoreNLP[4].

In model training, we set the dimension of the hidden state of the LSTM to 100, the dropout to 0.5, and the L2 regularization weight to 0.001. We use the Adam optimizer to optimize the model and set the batch size and the learning rate to 64 and 0.001 respectively.

4.3   Baseline Models

We use several models as our compared models, these baseline models are as follows:

Majority assigns the most frequent emotional polarity in the training set to each sample in the test set. TD-LSTM [2] uses two LSTM networks to model the left and right contexts with the target, which are stitched together as the final representation to predict the emotional polarity of the aspect. AE-LSTM [3] uses LSTM network to model context words, and combines the word hidden state with aspect embedding to supervise the generation of attention vectors. ATAE-LSTM [3] is based on the improvement of AE-LSTM. ATAE-LSTM further enhances the effect of aspect embedding, and adds aspect embedding after each word embedding vector to represent context. PosATT-LSTM [1] introduces position information to model the word's position, and then combines the hidden state of aspect and position information, supervising the generation of attention vectors.

MemNet [7] captures the correlation between each context word and the depicted aspect through multiple attentions, and focuses the last attention. IAN [8] uses two independent LSTM networks to model aspects and contexts respectively, and uses the average pooling of the hidden state of the context for aspect attention score calculation. RAM [9] is a multi-layer architecture, where each layer includes attention-based word feature aggregation and a GRU unit to learn sentence representation. SHAN [21] captures a synthesized global information and local information with gating mechanism by introducing a global attention score and a grammar-based local attention score respectively.

4.4   Experimental Results and Analysis

We test our model on the laptop and the restaurant datasets, the experimental results are shown in Table 2. As shown in Table 2, we can see that Majority has the worst effectiveness among all models. The LSTM-based models are better than Majority, which shows that LSTM network can effectively generate sentence feature representations to predict the emotional polarity of aspects.

---

[4] https://stanfordnlp.github.io/CoreNLP/.

Table 2. Experimental results of different models on the laptop and restaurant datasets.

Model	Laptop	Restaurant
Majority	53.45	65.00
TD-LSTM	68.13	75.63
AE-LSTM	68.90	76.20
ATAE-LSTM	68.70	77.20
MemNet	70.33	79.98
IAN	72.10	78.60
PosATT-LSTM	72.80	79.40
RAM	74.49	80.23
SHAN	74.64	81.02
Ours	**75.71**	**81.43**

We also can see that using the word position information related to the target plays an important role in generating the final representation. Both PosATT-LSTM and SHAN considered the positions of the words, and the experimental result of the two models are also remarkable. Comparing with ATAE-LSTM and PosATT-LSTM, we can see that PosATT-LSTM increased 4.1% and 2.2% performance in the laptop dataset and restaurant dataset, respectively by using location information. SHAN does not directly use the relative distance between each word and the aspect, but considers the distance based on the syntax, which eliminates a lot of noise to a certain extent and also achieves good results.

Our model combines relative distance and syntactic distance to further improve the performance of the experimental results. Compared with the above baseline models, our model achieve the best performance. In the laptop dataset and restaurant dataset, our model achieve 75.71% and 81.43% accuracy, respectively, which proves the feasibility of our model.

4.5 Ablation Studies

In order to verify the efficiency and advantage of different components of our proposed model, we also carried an ablation test. We use Pos-LSTM denotes that our model just retains the sentence encoding with position embedding without other components. We use Pos-Context-ATT denotes our model retain the context attention component, but without opinion attention component. The ablation test results are reported in Table 3.

Table 3. Experimental results of our model in ablation analysis.

Model	Laptop	Restaurant
Pos-LSTM	72.10	78.04
Pos-Context-ATT	74.45	79.82
Ours	75.71	81.43

As shown in Table 3, we can see that Pos-Context-ATT performs better than that of Pos-LSTM, which has an increase of 2.35% and 1.78% on laptop and restaurant datasets. This indicates that capturing the context information of words across sentence related to the target can actually improve the performance of this task. In addition, compared with Pos-Context-ATT, our final model has an increase of 1.26% and 1.61% on laptop and restaurant datasets, which means that the relationship between opinion words and the target is significantly supervised the final representation and improved the prediction results.

4.6 Discussion

To verify the impact of dependency distance of our model, we conducted several experiments with different dependency distances with 1, 2, and 3. The results are shown in Table 4.

Table 4. The impact analysis of dependency distance to our model.

Dependency distance	Laptop	Restaurant
1	**75.71**	**81.43**
2	74.76	80.62
3	73.51	79.64

It can be observed that the greater the dependency distance, the worse the per-formance of our model. Compared with the dependency distance of 1, when the dependency distance is 2, the accuracy decreases by 0.95% and 0.81%, and when the dependency distance is 3, the accuracy decreases by 2.2% and 1.79%. We believe that when the dependency distance is too large, it will choose opinion words that are not related to the aspect. And these opinion words introduce a lot of noise, which decrease the performance.

5 Conclusions

Basing on the observation that the independent relationship between opinion words and the target can supervise important sentimental information of the given target, a position-aware hybrid attention network for aspect-level sentiment analysis is proposed in this paper. Our model not only captures the context information of the words related to the target across the sentence, but also obtain the relationship between opinion words and the target. The experimental results carried on the public dataset show that our model is more effective than the compared baseline models.

Although hybrid attention proposed in our model achieve good performance, we find that the information of opinion attention is not well used in context attention. In the following research, we will focus on the interaction between the opinion words and the context of the content. We hope that opinion words are helpful to supervise the generation of attention scores in the context, which can make the model focus on context words related to opinion words.

Acknowledgements. This work is supported by National Nature Science Foundation of China (61976062), the Science and Technology Program of Guangzhou, China (No. 201904010303 and No. 202002030227) and the Special Funds for the Cultivation of Guangdong College Students' Scientific and Technological Innovation ("Climbing Program" Special Funds, grant number: pdjh2019b0173).

References

1. Zeng, J., Ma, X., Zhou, K.: Enhancing attention-based LSTM with position context for aspect-level sentiment classification. IEEE Access **7**, 20462–20471 (2019)
2. Tang, D., Qin, B., Feng, X., Liu, T.: Effective LSTMs for target-dependent sentiment classification. In: COLING 2016, pp. 3298–3307 (2016)
3. Wang, Y., Huang, M., Zhao, L., Zhu, X.: Attention-based LSTM for aspect-level sentiment classification. In: EMNLP 2016, pp. 606–615 (2016)
4. Kiritchenko, S., Zhu, X., Cherry, C., Mohammad, S.M.: Detecting aspects and sentiment in customer reviews. In: SemEval@COLING 2014, pp. 437–442 (2014)
5. Wagner, J., Arora, P., Cortes, S., Barman, U., Bogdanova, D., Foster, J., Tounsi, L.: Aspect-based polarity classification for SemEval task 4. In: SemEval@COLING 2014, pp. 223–229 (2014)
6. Vo, D.-T., Zhang, Y.: Target-dependent twitter sentiment classification with rich automatic features. In: IJCAI 2015, pp. 1347–1353 (2015)
7. Tang, D., Qin, B., Liu, T.: Aspect level sentiment classification with deep memory network. In: EMNLP 2016, pp. 214–224 (2016)
8. Ma, D., Li, S., Zhang, X., Wang, H.: Interactive attention networks for aspect-level sentiment classification. In: IJCAI 2017, pp. 4068–4074 (2017)
9. Chen, P., Sun, Z., Bing, L., Yang, W.: Recurrent attention network on memory for aspect sentiment analysis. In: EMNLP 2017, pp. 452–461 (2017)
10. Vaswani, A., et al.: Attention is all you need. In: NIPS 2017, pp. 5998–6008 (2017)
11. Zheng, S., Xia, R.: Left-center-right separated neural network for aspect-based sentiment analysis with rotatory attention. CoRR abs/1802.00892 (2018)
12. Tay, Y., Tuan, L.A., Hui, S.C.: Learning to attend via word-aspect associative fusion for aspect-based sentiment analysis. In: AAAI 2018, pp. 5956–5963 (2018)
13. Huang, B., Ou, Y., Carley, K.M.: Aspect level sentiment classification with attention-over-attention neural networks. In: SBP-BRiMS 2018, pp. 197–206 (2018)
14. Xue W, Li T.: Aspect Based Sentiment Analysis with Gated Convolutional Networks.. In: ACL 2018. Association for Computational Linguistics, vol. 1, pp. 2514–2523 (2018)
15. Liu, F., Cohn, T., Baldwin, T.: Recurrent entity networks with delayed memory update for targeted aspect-based sentiment analysis. In: NAACL-HLT 2018, vol. 2, pp. 278–283 (2018)
16. Majumder, N., Poria, S., Gelbukh, A., Akhtar, S., Cambria, E., Ekbal, A.: IARM: inter-aspect relation modeling with memory networks in aspect-based sentiment analysis. In: EMNLP 2018, pp. 3402–3411 (2018)
17. Wu, S., Xu, Y., Wu, F., Yuan, Z., Huang, Y., Li, X.: Aspect-based sentiment analysis via fusing multiple sources of textual knowledge. Knowl. Based Syst. **183**, 104868 (2019)

18. Liang, B., Du, J., Xu, R., Li, B., Huang, H.: Context-aware embedding for targeted aspect-based sentiment analysis. In: ACL 2019, vol. 1, pp. 4678–4683 (2019)
19. Bao, L., Lambert, P., Badia, T.: Attention and lexicon regularized LSTM for aspect-based sentiment analysis. In: ACL 2019, vol. 2, pp. 253–259 (2019)
20. He, R., Lee, W.S., Ng, H.T., Dahlmeier, D.: An interactive multi-task learning network for end-to-end aspect-based sentiment analysis. In: ACL 2019, vol.1, pp. 504–515 (2019)
21. Wang, X., Xu, G., Zhang, J., Sun, X., Wang, L., Huang, T.: Syntax-directed hybrid attention network for aspect-level sentiment analysis. IEEE Access 7, 5014–5025 (2019)
22. Li, L., Liu, Y., Zhou, A.: Hierarchical attention based position-aware network for aspect-level sentiment analysis. In: CoNLL 2018, pp. 181–189 (2018)
23. Hu, M., Liu, B.: Mining and summarizing customer reviews. In: KDD 2004, pp. 168–177 (2004)
24. Pennington, J., Socher, R., Manning, C.D.: GloVe: global vectors for word representation. In: EMNLP 2014, pp. 1532–1543 (2014)
25. Mikolov, T., Chen, K., Corrado, G., Dean, J.: Distributed representations of words and phrases and their compositionality. In: NIPS 2013, pp. 3111–3119 (2013)
26. Hochreiter, S., Urgen Schmidhuber, J.: Long short-term memory. Neural Comput. 9(8), 1735–1780 (1997)

IR in Finance

An Integrated Machine Learning Framework for Stock Price Prediction

Quanzhi Bi[1], Hongfei Yan[1,3]($\boxtimes$), Chong Chen[2], and Qi Su[1]

[1] Peking University, Beijing, People's Republic of China
{biquanzhi,yanhf,sukia}@pku.edu.cn
[2] Beijing Normal University, Beijing, People's Republic of China
chenchong@pku.edu.cn
[3] National Engineering Laboratory for Big Data Analysis and Application Technology, Center for Big Data Research, Peking University, Beijing, People's Republic of China

Abstract. Predicting the future price of financial assets has always been an important research topic in the field of quantitative finance. This paper attempts to use the latest artificial intelligence technologies to design and implement a framework for financial asset price prediction. The framework we use is divided into three modules: Feature Engineering, Regressor, and Hyper Optimizer. The Feature Engineering module extract multiple features using technical indicators, FinBERT, FFT, ARIMA, stacked auto-encoder, PCA and XGBoost. The Regressor module consists of a generative adversarial network, where the generator is Seq2Seq and the discriminator is GRU. The HyperOptimizer module will tune the parameter in GAN using the Bayesian optimization algorithm. Finally, we conducted numerical experiments on our framework, which shows that the framework implemented in this paper performs better than the benchmark method.

Keywords: Stock prediction · Stacked autoencoder · NLP · GAN · Bayesian optimization

1 Introduction

Predicting the future price of financial assets has always been an important research topic in the field of quantitative finance, and is often the focus of researchers from hedge funds, investment banks and other financial technology institutions. Due to the high complexity of financial markets and the large number of people involved in trading, rigorous mathematical modelling of secondary trading markets for financial assets is difficult, and price prediction models based

Supported by: NSFC Grant 61772044; MSTC Grant 2019YFC1521203: research, development and demonstration of key technologies for knowledge organization and services for Antiques based on Knowledge Graph; Peking University Grant 2020: "New Ideas for Teaching 2.0" key project.

on these methods have difficulty capturing the pattern of change. However, on the other hand, the volume of data in the financial markets has become increasingly large with the increasing storage and computing power of computers, and in recent years, machine learning based on data has developed rapidly, deriving many advanced algorithms to predict time series. This article attempts to use these latest artificial intelligence technologies to predict the prices of multiple equity underpinnings of US stocks.

Building a predictive framework for financial assets often has many difficulties in the past, including too many methods to predict asset prices, which are difficult to integrate into one framework, difficulty in extracting features of deep learning algorithms from historical price data and text-based fundamental data in the market, which is difficult to quantify, and manual extraction of features is often time-consuming and laborious and not comprehensive enough, time series prediction has been the shortcoming of machine learning algorithms due to the existence of serial autocorrelation, deep learning algorithms often have a large number of parameters, difficulty in tuning, etc. In response to the above-mentioned difficulties, the main tasks of this paper are as follows.

1. Implemented and improved the framework for financial asset price forecasting, the raw idea was originally proposed by [3].
2. Integrates multiple traditional technical indicators.
3. Combines a characteristic mix of underlying assets, including commodities, currencies, indices, VIX, and more.
4. Uses the latest NLP model FinBERT[2] to conduct sentiment analysis of financial-related news in the market.
5. Uses Fourier transform techniques to extract the overall trend of price changes.
6. Extract of asset price similarity using traditional ARIMA model.
7. Uses Stacked Autoencoders to identify other advanced features.
8. Uses principal component analysis PCA to create feature portfolios to reduce the number of dimensions of features created by the self-coder.
9. Uses the currently most popular statistical learning model, XGBoost[1] to analyze feature importance.
10. Forecasts asset prices using the generative adversarial network GAN, where the generator is the latest Seq2Seq and the discriminator is GRU.
11. Uses the Bayesian optimization algorithm BOA for GAN tuning, resulting in a significant reduction in tuning time.
12. tests 147 select US stocks.

2   Related Work

Deep learning is a representation learning method based on artificial neural network architecture, which can transform data into features of machine learning

---

[1] In recent years, the XGBoost algorithm has been used frequently in data science competitions and is one of the most popular machine learning algorithms.

algorithms, avoiding the step of manual feature extraction from the beginning, reducing the difficulty of algorithm development while increasing the complexity of the model. Also deep learning has a very low generalization error [14] that is not reached by the traditional statistical learning methods, thus making breakthroughs in various fields, including image processing [13], natural language processing [10], time series prediction [4], etc.

Among them, the most popular approach in the time series prediction problem is a variant of the recurrent neural network RNN, where the most used model is the long and short term memory LSTM [9], a recurrent neural network that can fluctuate long-time data. For example [5] studied the application of LSTM in the Chinese market, on top of LSTM, [7] added the extreme event memory unit with extreme event loss function, so that the model can learn and predict extreme changes in asset prices. [1] used bidirectional LSTM to predict short and long-term stock returns. [16] proposes the State Frequency Memory (SFM) recurrent network, where each unit is decomposed with a discrete Fourier transform DFT on the basis of a recurrent neural network to extract laws at different frequencies.

In 2014 the generative adversarial network [8] was proposed, which is a semi-supervised learning method that consists of two neural networks against each other, one of which is called a generator, and the goal is to mimic the distribution of the training sample by randomly sampling from the potential space and sending it to another neural network called a discriminator, which discriminates whether the sample belongs to the distribution of the training sample. GAN has also been attempted to be applied to time series prediction. [17] uses GAN to predict the Chinese stock index, where the generator is LSTM and the discriminator is CNN, and the input data are one-dimensional price series. [15] uses GAN to forecast the closing price of the S&P 500 and some US stocks, the generator is LSTM and the discriminator is MLP.

With the development of deep learning, natural language processing techniques are also advancing rapidly, making more accurate news sentiment analysis possible. Natural language processing is the use of computers to analyze and express human language, mainly in the areas of text classification, sentiment analysis, text generation, etc. In the asset price forecasting problem, we need to quantitatively analyze the impact that media has on asset price changes, so we are mainly concerned with text classification and sentiment analysis applications. Wherein [11] proposes the Recursive Neural Tensor Network (RNTN), which expands the learning capacity of a neural network by adding a tensor layer to the unit of the RNN. [12] proposed an attentional mechanism-based LSTM to classify the emotions of texts at the aspect level of granularity. 2018 Google proposed the pre-trained model BERT [6], Bidirectional Encoder Representations from Transformers, which is a bidirectional encoder representation from Transformer that pre-trains deep bidirectional representations based on the left and right contexts of all layers, allowing more accurate analysis of the emotion values of texts.

3   Methods

The model framework we use is divided into three modules: Feature Engineering, Regressor and Hyper Optimizer, in which the Feature Engineering module is subdivided into Feature Extraction and Feature Reprocessing (Auto Encoder, PCA, XGB), as shown in Fig. 1.

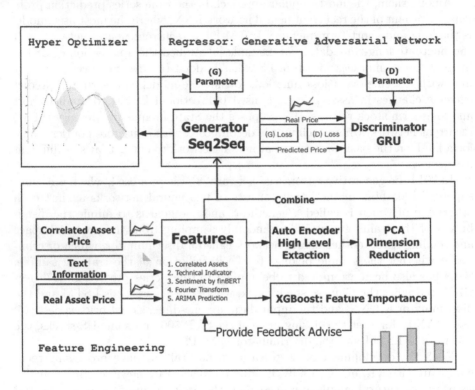

Fig. 1. Financial asset price prediction model framework

3.1   Feature Engineering

After inputting various asset historical price and news data, the feature extraction module first pre-processes the raw data and calculates some artificially defined feature sequences, which require researchers to conduct continuous research and experimentation, here this paper attempts to extract several features that are more popular in academia and industry, namely: relevant asset prices, some traditional technical indicators, sentiment values of relevant news, Fourier variation extracted trend features of different frequency domains, and the results of prediction using the ARIMA model, a total of five categories of features. After that we use stacked auto-encoder to extract higher-level features and then use PCA to reduce the dimension. The researcher can have feedback of the extracted features by XGBoost. A full description of the extracted features has been listed in Table 1.

3.2   Regressor

After we have extracted useful features, we need a regressor model to learn the nonlinear relationship between features and asset prices, i.e., a nonlinear function approximator to fit the feature-to-price mapping function, traditional methods generally use simple linear regression models or statistical learning models, which either have good statistical explanatory power or some nonlinear fitting ability, but with the continuous development of artificial intelligence technology, deep learning is starting to be widely used by industry and academia. We use the generative adversarial network as a regressor here, where the generator is Seq2Seq and the discriminator is GRU. The parameter setting can be found in Table 3.

3.3   Hyper Optimizer

Machine learning models usually have a lot of hyperparameters such as learning rate, structure of neural network, etc. that their algorithm's built-in SGD optimization cannot handle, so using machine learning methods requires a lot of time to tune the parameters, which is a bottomneck in the financial asset price prediction problem, because the market changes quickly and the computer algorithm we designed needs to give the prediction results in a very short time for the trading system to process. Here, we apply the Bayesian Optimization Algorithm BOA (Bayesian Optimization Algorithm) to fine-tune the regressor.

4   Experiment

4.1   Dataset

The price data used in this experiment mainly comes from Yahoo Finance[2], downloaded by Python API, while the news data comes from SeekingAlpha[3], this paper uses the news data[4] of 147 selected U.S. stocks pre-crawled and cleaned by the SEWM group of Peking University. Its stock code is shown in Table 2.

---

[2] https://finance.yahoo.com.
[3] https://seekingalpha.com/market-news.
[4] https://github.com/zeyazhang/sewm_stock_data/blob/master/UsStockNews.rar.

Table 1. All features extracted by feature engineering module

Feature code	Feature explanation
High	Highest price in the last trading session
Low	Lowest price in the last trading session
Open	Opening price during the last trading session
Close	Closing price in the last trading session
Volume	Volume in the previous trading session
Adj Close	Post-market closure adjusted closing price
JPM	Related Assets: JPM share price
MS	Related Assets: Morgan Stanley Share Price
LIBOR	LIBOR (market rate)
VIX	CBOE Volatility Index
SS Close	SSE Composite Index Closing Price
DJI Close	Dow Jones Industrials Closing Price
IXIC Close	NASDAQ Composite Index Closing Price
GSPC Close	S&P 500 Index Closing Price
N225 Close	Nikkei Average Closing Price
HSI Close	Hong Kong Hang Seng Index Closing Price
FCHI Close	Paris Securities Union Index Closing Price
GDAXI Close	German DAX Closing Price
DEXJPUS	Exchange rate: JPY/USD
DEXCHUS	Exchange rate: RMB/USD
MA7	7-day simple moving average
MA21	21-day simple moving average
26ema	26-day moving average of the index
12ema	12-day moving average of the index
MACD	Moving average convergence/divergence
20sd	Bollinger bands mid-rail
upper_band	Bollinger band upper track
Lower_band	Bollinger Band lower track
EMA	Exponential moving average
Momentum	Momentum Indicators
log_momentum	Logarithmic momentum indicator
Sentiment	Sentiment value of financial news
Fourier 3	DFT 3-order reconstruction
Fourier 6	DFT 6-order reconstruction
Fourier 9	DFT 9-order reconstruction
ARIMA	ARIMA model prediction
PCA1	(PCA component) extracted by stack autoencoder
PCA2	(PCA component) extracted by stack autoencoder
PCA3	(PCA component) extracted by stack autoencoder
PCA4	(PCA component) extracted by stack autoencoder
PCA5	(PCA component) extracted by stack autoencoder

Table 2. Stock code to be tested

Stock Market	U.S.
Numer of Stocks	147
Starting Date	2012-9-4
Ending Date	2016-10-31
Train/Test Separation Date	2015-12-28
Number of Trading Days	1048

AAL	AVP	CHNR	DD	GD	HSY	MDT	PEP	SO	UTX
AAPL	AXP	CHT	DIS	GE	IBM	MET	PFE	SPIL	VOD
AA	BABA	CI	DSX	GIGM	INTC	MMM	PG	S	V
ABT	BAC	CL	DUK	GM	IP	MO	QCOM	TGT	VZ
ADBE	BA	CMCSA	EBAY	GOOG	JD	MRK	RF	TM	WFC
ADS	BAX	COF	EDU	GS	JNJ	MSFT	ROK	T	WMB
AEP	BIDU	COP	EL	HAL	JOBS	MS	RTN	TSLA	WMT
AES	BK	COV	EMC	HD	JPM	NKE	SBUX	TSM	WY
AIG	BMY	CPB	EP	HIG	JRJC	NOK	SHI	TWX	XIN
ALL	CAT	C	ERIC	HIMX	KMI	NSC	SIMO	TXN	XOM
AMGN	CBS	CSCO	ETR	HMC	KO	NTES	SINA	UMC	XRX
AMZN	CCU	CTSH	EXC	HNP	LFC	NWS	SLB	UNH	ZNH
APA	CEA	CVS	FDX	HNZ	MA	NYX	SLE	UPS	
ASX	CEO	CVX	F	HON	MAT	ORCL	SNP	USB	
ATI	CHA	CYD	GCI	HPQ	MCD	OXY	SOHU	UTSI	

4.2 Expriment Setup

The objectives of the experiment in this chapter are to answer the following questions.

RQ1: What is the statistical nature of the feature engineering module, e.g. correlation, etc. To study **RQ1**, we compute a correlation matrix for the feature vector of each subject and then count the number of features with correlation coefficients higher than 0.9 (recorded as the repeatability index), and we determine which features have strong correlation (repeatability) by computing the average correlation coefficient index for all subjects.

RQ2: Whether the regressor module is valid. To study **RQ2**, we make price predictions for all the subject, in which we select the first 7 days as input data to predict prices for the following year, and we define a metric (RMSPE, see next section) to measure the validity of the model ourselves, without using the HyperOptimizer module first.

RQ3: whether the regressor module can exceed the existing baseline model. To study **RQ3**, we use the benchmark model to make price predictions

Table 3. Experimental parameter setting

Parameter symbols	Parameter explanations	Selected values
EMA(α)	Calculate the weight of the moving average of the index	$\alpha = 0.5$
BB(N, K)	Window size and volatility size	N = 20, K = 2
Sentiment	FinBERT analysis of sentiment	Average of sentiment per day
ARIMA(p, d, q)	AR order p, difference order d, MA order q	p = 3, d = 1, q = 2
SdA n_hidden	Number of stacked self-encoder hidden layers	400
SdA n_latent	Stack self-encoder latent layer number	2
SdA n_layers	Stack self-encoder network layers	3
SdA learning_rate	Stack self-encoder Adam learning rate	0.01
SdA epoch	Stack self encoder training wheels	150
PCA	PCA interpretation ratio	80%
Seq2Seq embedding1	Seq2Seq embedding1	42 × 64
Seq2Seq embedding2	Seq2Seq embedding layer2	64 × 64
Seq2Seq encoder	Seq2Seq encoding layer	GRU(64,64,2)
Seq2Seq decoder	Seq2Seq decoder	GRU(64,64,2)
Seq2Seq drop	Seq2Seq dropout probability	0.2
D GRU	Identifier GRU structure	GUR(1,32,2)
GAN length	GAN using the previous length day to predict the next day	7
GAN batchsize	GAN batch size	32
BOA init_points	Bayesian optimization algorithm initial sample size	5
BOA n_iter	Bayesian Optimization Iteration Number	25
BOA lr	GAN optimization algorithm learning rate range	[0.001,0.005]
BOA epoch	GAN optimized epoch quantity range	[100,150]
BOA acq	Bayesian optimal sampling function	acq = ucb
BOA kappa	Bayesian optimized Gaussian process variance	kappa = 2.576

for the aforementioned assets, and here we use the traditional method ARIMA$(3, 1, 2)$ (already calculated at the time of feature calculation) for comparison.

RQ4: whether the HyperOptimizer module has a significant effect. To study **RQ4**, we added the HyperOptimizer module to see if the performance of our model got significantly better.

Table 3 shows the hyperparameters that need to be set for this experiment. The outcome metric used in this paper is RMSPE (Root mean squared Percentage Error), which is the ratio of RMSE to the mean of the predicted value p_t.

$$\text{RMSPE} = \frac{\sqrt{\text{mean}(e_t^2)}}{\text{mean}(|p_t|)} \tag{1}$$

The main benefit of this method is its scale-free nature, i.e. we can compare uniformly regardless of the predicted price of p_t at what price level.

4.3   Experiment Result

The results of the statistical analysis of the feature data are shown in Fig. 4b, and we can see that, except for the OHLC data, which are inherently reproducible, the rest of the features do not have a high reproducibility index, so we can answer **RQ1** that the features we extract are of a good statistical nature (Fig. 2).

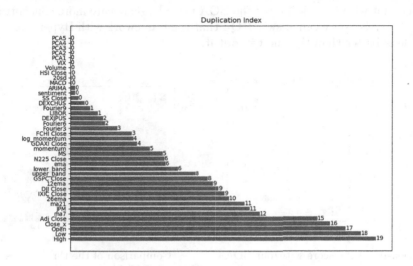

Fig. 2. Reproducibility index of extracted features

The results of our framework run on GS (example) are shown in Fig. 3 and the results on all assets are shown in Fig. 4b. We can see that it performs well and its RMSPE is averaged around 2.95%, i.e., it can predict the next day's financial asset price with a margin of error of 5%, so we can answer **RQ2** and **RQ3**, i.e., our framework is valid and exceeds the benchmark model ARIMA.

Fig. 3. Prediction result of GS

The experimental results of the BOA module are shown in Table 4, where the bolded part is the part with improved performance. Our results show that the vast majority of the subjects have achieved significantly better results through tonal participation, with a mean RMSPE of 1.63%, a decrease compared to the result without BOA participation, and the KDE distribution comparison can be found in Fig. 4a while the final score comparison can be found in Fig. 4b. We can see that with the addition of the BOA module, scores are more concentrated at lower levels, so we can answer **RQ4** that the framework with HyperOptimizer module is better than the one without it.

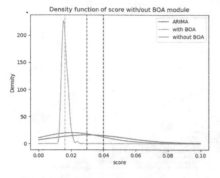
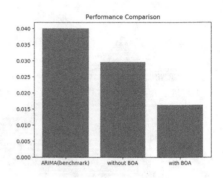

Density of the score with/out BOA   Comparison of the three scores

Fig. 4. Final performance

Table 4. Expriment result of the framework (with BOA)

Code	Score	Code	Score	Code	Score	Code	Score	Code	Score
GOOG	**0.014**	BIDU	**0.016**	MSFT	**0.014**	AAPL	**0.015**	GS	0.015
UTSI	**0.016**	WMT	**0.016**	BABA	**0.017**	PEP	0.015	XOM	**0.014**
BA	0.018	NKE	**0.016**	QCOM	**0.015**	APA	**0.017**	SBUX	**0.014**
AVP	**0.015**	HSY	**0.016**	MAT	**0.015**	GCI	**0.017**	SNP	**0.016**
SOHU	**0.018**	OXY	**0.013**	KMI	**0.015**	UPS	0.016	FDX	**0.017**
DSX	**0.023**	AAL	**0.017**	NTES	**0.014**	SINA	**0.018**	EDU	**0.019**
JD	**0.017**	JRJC	**0.014**	AMZN	**0.013**	INTC	**0.018**	IBM	0.015
EBAY	**0.016**	ORCL	0.016	TXN	**0.013**	CSCO	0.018	C	**0.016**
BAC	**0.015**	JPM	**0.013**	MS	**0.014**	AIG	0.018	JNJ	0.016
PFE	0.016	KO	0.015	MDT	**0.016**	ABT	0.020	COP	**0.015**
SLB	**0.014**	DUK	0.014	HMC	**0.015**	TM	0.017	TSLA	**0.013**
GE	**0.014**	PG	0.016	EL	0.020	GD	**0.018**	CL	0.014
DD	**0.014**	T	0.015	HPQ	**0.016**	S	**0.015**	ERIC	**0.017**
XRX	**0.014**	VOD	**0.015**	ADS	**0.015**	CTSH	**0.015**	NOK	**0.018**
ADBE	**0.016**	EMC	**0.014**	VZ	0.021	USB	**0.016**	RF	**0.014**
V	0.018	BK	0.018	WFC	**0.014**	MET	0.018	ALL	0.015
HIG	**0.017**	NYX	**0.015**	AXP	**0.016**	MA	**0.016**	CI	**0.017**

(contniued)

Table 4. *(contniued)*

COF	**0.014**	BMY	**0.016**	MO	**0.016**	UNH	**0.015**	MRK	0.016
AMGN	0.017	CVS	**0.015**	BAX	0.017	CPB	0.019	HNZ	**0.015**
MCD	0.016	SLE	**0.015**	GM	**0.015**	F	**0.014**	CVX	0.013
CAT	**0.017**	HAL	**0.013**	AES	**0.013**	WMB	**0.015**	SO	0.020
EP	**0.017**	ETR	0.018	EXC	**0.014**	AEP	0.017	TWX	**0.019**
DIS	**0.013**	CCU	**0.018**	NWS	0.015	CBS	**0.013**	CMCSA	0.015
AA	**0.015**	HON	**0.015**	RTN	**0.016**	MMM	0.015	HD	**0.016**
ROK	0.015	IP	**0.018**	TGT	**0.016**	ATI	**0.014**	NSC	**0.014**
WY	0.015	UTX	0.015	CYD	**0.017**	CEO	**0.018**	HNP	**0.014**
ZNH	**0.015**	SHI	**0.018**	JOBS	**0.014**	CHNR	**0.015**	LFC	**0.016**
XIN	**0.014**	CEA	**0.013**	CHA	**0.015**	ASX	**0.014**	CHT	0.014
TSM	0.019	HIMX	**0.015**	UMC	0.019	SPIL	**0.016**	SIMO	**0.017**
GIGM	**0.015**								

5   Conclusion

The main work and conclusions of this paper are as follows.

1. Implements and improves upon the framework proposed by [3], where the improvements are: using FinBERT, using SeqSeq, running multiple underlying assets, etc.
2. Uses data from Yahoo Finance and SeekingAlpha, combined with the latest AI technology and traditional methods, extracted a number of artificial and deep-seated characteristics, including related assets, technical indicators, sentiment values, DFT, ARIMA, and used SdA and principal component analysis for dimension reduction.
3. Uses GAN to learn and predict the generated feature sequences, incorporating sequence processing techniques such as SeqSeq and GRU, which have become more popular in recent years.
4. Uses a Bayesian optimization technique to perform global black-box tuning of the GAN parameters, achieving a rapid implementation of hyperparameter tuning.
5. Numerical experiments on 147 U.S. stocks were conducted to verify the validity of our proposed feature engineering module, regressor module, and hyper optimizer module. Our module has been proved to out-perform the benchmark.

References

1. Althelaya, K.A., El-Alfy, E.S.M., Mohammed, S.: Evaluation of bidirectional LSTM for short-and long-term stock market prediction. In: 2018 9th International Conference on Information and Communication Systems (ICICS), pp. 151–156. IEEE (2018)

2. Araci, D.: FinBERT: financial sentiment analysis with pre-trained language models. arXiv preprint arXiv:1908.10063 (2019)
3. Banushev, B.: borisbanushev/stockpredictionai (2020). https://github.com/borisbanushev/stockpredictionai
4. Brownlee, J.: Deep Learning for Time Series Forecasting: Predict the Future with MLPs. CNNs and LSTMs in Python, Machine Learning Mastery (2018)
5. Chen, K., Zhou, Y., Dai, F.: A LSTM-based method for stock returns prediction: a case study of China stock market. In: 2015 IEEE International Conference on Big Data (Big Data), pp. 2823–2824. IEEE (2015)
6. Devlin, J., Chang, M.W., Lee, K., Toutanova, K.: BERT: pre-training of deep bidirectional transformers for language understanding. arXiv preprint arXiv:1810.04805 (2018)
7. Ding, D., Zhang, M., Pan, X., Yang, M., He, X.: Modeling extreme events in time series prediction. In: Proceedings of the 25th ACM SIGKDD International Conference on Knowledge Discovery & Data Mining, pp. 1114–1122 (2019)
8. Goodfellow, I., Bengio, Y., Courville, A.: Deep Learning. MIT Press, Cambridge (2016)
9. Hochreiter, S., Schmidhuber, J.: Long short-term memory. Neural Comput. **9**(8), 1735–1780 (1997)
10. Socher, R., Bengio, Y., Manning, C.D.: Deep learning for NLP (without magic). In: Tutorial Abstracts of ACL 2012, p. 5. Association for Computational Linguistics (2012)
11. Socher, R., Perelygin, A., Wu, J., Chuang, J., Manning, C.D., Ng, A.Y., Potts, C.: Recursive deep models for semantic compositionality over a sentiment treebank. In: Proceedings of the 2013 Conference on Empirical Methods in Natural Language Processing, pp. 1631–1642 (2013)
12. Wang, Y., Huang, M., Zhu, X., Zhao, L.: Attention-based LSTM for aspect-level sentiment classification. In: Proceedings of the 2016 Conference on Empirical Methods in Natural Language Processing, pp. 606–615 (2016)
13. Wu, R., Yan, S., Shan, Y., Dang, Q., Sun, G.: Deep image: scaling up image recognition. arXiv preprint arXiv:1501.02876 7(8) (2015)
14. Zhang, C., Bengio, S., Hardt, M., Recht, B., Vinyals, O.: Understanding deep learning requires rethinking generalization. arXiv preprint arXiv:1611.03530 (2016)
15. Zhang, K., Zhong, G., Dong, J., Wang, S., Wang, Y.: Stock market prediction based on generative adversarial network. Procedia Comput. Sci. **147**, 400–406 (2019)
16. Zhang, L., Aggarwal, C., Qi, G.J.: Stock price prediction via discovering multi-frequency trading patterns. In: Proceedings of the 23rd ACM SIGKDD International Conference on Knowledge Discovery and Data Mining, pp. 2141–2149 (2017)
17. Zhou, X., Pan, Z., Hu, G., Tang, S., Zhao, C.: Stock market prediction on high-frequency data using generative adversarial nets. Math. Probl. Eng. **2018** (2018). 11 p.

Empirical Research on Futures Trading Strategy Based on Time Series Algorithm

Shi Yao[1]([✉]), Yan Hongfei[1,3] [iD], Ying Siping[1] [iD], Chen Chong[2] [iD], and Su Qi[1] [iD]

[1] Peking University, Beijing, People's Republic of China
{shall,fyanhf,sukiag}@pku.edu.cn, spying0403g@gmail.com
[2] Beijing Normal University, Beijing, People's Republic of China
chenchong@pku.edu.cn
[3] National Engineering Laboratory for Big Data Analysis and Application Technology, Center for Big Data Research, Peking University, Beijing, People's Republic of China

Abstract. This article attempts to establish a trading strategy framework based on deep neural networks for the futures market, which consists of two parts: time series forecasting and trading strategies based on trading signals. In the time series forecasting task, we experimented with three types of methods with different entry points, namely recurrent neural networks with gate structure, networks combining time and frequency domain information, and network structures using attention mechanism. In the trading strategy part, the buying and selling signals and the corresponding trading volume are established according to the prediction results, and trading is conducted with the frequency of hours. In the empirical exploration part, we tested the prediction effect and strategic rate of return of various models on the copper contract. The data shows that in general, the best strategy can obtain a relatively stable income growth that has nothing to do with market fluctuations, but lacks countermeasures for rare external events with greater impact.

Keywords: Futures · Quantitative trading · Deep neural network · Long short-term memory network · Attention mechanism

1 Introduction

Futures are financial contracts that involve the sale of financial instruments or physical commodities for future delivery and are mainly divided into commodity futures and financial futures. A futures contract is a contract for the purchase and sale of futures, and is an agreement between two parties to trade at a specific time when the buyer needs to acquire a specified asset at a specific price

Peking University Grant 2020: "New Ideas for Teaching 2.0" Key Project; MSTC Grant 2019YFC1521203: research, development and demonstration of key technologies for knowledge organization and services for Antiques based on Knowledge Graph; NSFC Grant 61772044.

© Springer Nature Switzerland AG 2020
Z. Dou et al. (Eds.): CCIR 2020, LNCS 12285, pp. 111–123, 2020.
https://doi.org/10.1007/978-3-030-56725-5_9

(also known as the delivery date), the seller delivers the asset at that price, and the asset in exchange is called the underlying. For the same underlying, the futures exchange specifies multiple delivery months, each corresponding to a futures contract, while the main contract represents the highest volume contract. Futures trading is a two-way trading mechanism where buyers and sellers are called long and short respectively.

Through statistical and mathematical methods and computer programming, quantitative trading is based on a large amount of historical data to predict the future market, and follows the probability of formulating the corresponding trading strategy, according to the rules of automated buying and selling operations, in order to seek a stable and high return above the average return.

CTA (commodity trading advisor) generally refers to the investment in futures asset management products, mainly divided into trend strategy and arbitrage strategy, the former occupies the mainstream position. The trend strategy refers to tracking the market trend, going long or short, and is divided into long-term trend tracking strategy, medium-term trend tracking strategy and short-term intraday trend tracking strategy.

Currently, most of the work on financial time series forecasting using deep learning focuses on stock price and index price forecasting, and less work on commodity prices and futures prices [1]. This paper focuses on short-term intraday trend tracking strategies through the method of deep learning to predict prices based on historical data, so as to achieve the effect of tracking the market trend, and in this way to generate buying and selling signals to achieve trading strategies.

2   Time Series Prediction Methods

The futures trading strategy in this paper is based on time series single-step prediction results, and the specific methods used will be described in this chapter.

2.1   Long- and Short-Term Memory Networks

Recurrent neural networks (RNN) were first proposed by David E. Rumelhart et al. in 1986 [2] to apply deep neural networks to the processing of sequence data. The key idea of RNN is that different parts of the model can share parameters through the loop connection of hidden units in adjacent moments, so that the network can be conveniently extended to longer sequences, and also has the ability to process longer sequences, but the gradient disappears or the gradient explodes as the time series grows during training [3]. Hochreiter and Schmidhuber proposed the Long Short-Term Memory Network (LSTM) in 1997 [4], which alleviated the above problems to a certain extent, and the practical results showed very good results and robustness, with great success in tasks such as speech recognition [5] and machine translation [6].

2.2   Methodology Incorporating Frequency Domain Characteristics

LSTM has alleviated the problem of long-distance dependence to some extent, but has not solved it. In order to obtain information about different trends, a class of methods attempts to obtain data of different granularity representing trends across different spans through hierarchical modeling. Koutník et al. [9] divide the hidden layers of the RNN into different modules that are responsible for extracting information only for fixed periods. Chang et al. [10] freely combine different RNN units based on multi-resolution jump connections. Cui et al. [11] propose a CNN network structure at multiple scales. Chung et al. [12] propose an RNN network structure at multiple scales, but also mention that there is no evidence that models of this class can actually capture information across long time spans.

The frequency domain is a coordinate system that describes the fluctuating characteristics of the cycle of things. In general, time series predictions are made based on the time domain. In this paper, we have used the discrete Wavelet transform to modify RNN for the futures price prediction task(wLSTM).

Wavelet transform was proposed by S.G. Mallat in 1989 [17]. Figure 1 gives the network structure of mLSTM after three decompositions. After three decompositions, the final result is a three-stage high-pass filtering result and a final low-pass filtering result. The sequence length after each decomposition is reduced by half due to downsampling, the former is mainly used to obtain frequency domain information, while the latter is used to represent time domain details. Finally, the decomposition results are passed through the LSTM and the output is concated together.

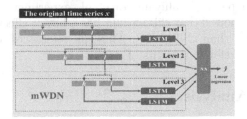

Fig. 1. mLSTM [16]

2.3   Methods of Introducing Attention Mechanisms

The attention mechanism, proposed by Dzmitry Bahdanau et al. in 2015 [18], breaks the limitation of fixed intermediate vectors in end-to-end structures, called bahdanau attention, and is widely used in various types of networks, yielding many variants [19]. During the step-by-step processing of the input sequence by the encoder, all intermediate output results are retained in the context vector. In each step of the encoding, the similarity between the input of the step and the output of the encoder is calculated separately, which is weighted to obtain the context vector of the step and participate in the calculation together. Attentional mechanisms can likewise be introduced in single-step time series prediction tasks, and long-distance dependencies can be captured directly through this mechanism.

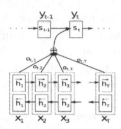

Fig. 2. Bahdanau attention [18]

Ashish Vaswani et al. proposed the Transformer model in 2017 [20], which ditches the traditional RNN structure and deals with sequence problems based entirely on attentional mechanisms, more directly acquiring information over long distances, while improving parallelism. The model employs an encoder-decoder structure.

Considering that the task of this paper is single-step time series prediction, which does not require the use of end-to-end structures, and the amount of data is insufficient to support an overly complex model, a variant of the decoder in Transformer will be used. Shiyang Li et al. experimented with artificially generated data and showed that this variant has a better effect in capturing long sequence information than LSTM [21]. Thus, all references to the Transformer in the following text refer to variants of its decoder.

3   Empirical Analysis

3.1   Data Pre-processing

The subject matter of this article is the copper contract from the Shanghai Futures Exchange, which is a large Chinese futures exchange. Data covers the period from 1 January 2005 to 18 February 2020.

After identifying the subject matter, we need to select the granularity of the data. There's a certain trade-off in terms of data granularity. For data volatility, measured by calculating the standard deviation of the percentage change in the closing price, the statistics are given in Table 1, the model used is considered in a comprehensive manner, the 60-min level of data is selected, and closing price is used.

Table 1. Data characteristics at different data granularities

Frequency	15 min	60 min	1 day
Standard deviation (%)	0.45	0.80	1.24
Data volume	78244	19561	3675

On the dataset division, considering the problem of information leakage after time series disruption, we use the HOLDOUT method to divide the dataset chronologically. To better measure the performance of the algorithm under different scenarios, we used 3 contracts as the test set, during which the market has successively gone through three phases: uptrend, sustained volatility and downtrend. The validation set is also 3 contracts.

Data from the remaining contracts were added to the experiment for pre-training. However, some screening of varieties is required because of the potentially very significant differences in markets between varieties, which violates the independent homodistribution assumptions. Table 2 gives the Pearson correlation coefficients between copper contracts and individual contracts. Through this indicator, the aluminum contract (Al) and rebar contract (Rb) were finally selected as the pre-training dataset.

Table 2. Correlation of each contract with copper contracts

Contract	Ag	Al	Au	Bu	Fu	Hc
Correlation factor	−0.19	0.71	1.24	−0.30	0.52	−0.06
Contract	Ni	Pb	Rb	Sn	Wr	Zn
Correlation factor	−0.06	−0.57	−0.80	0.01	−0.07	−0.44

3.2 Trading Strategy Setting

Based on the predicted closing price for the next hour and the current price, a buy signal is generated if the prediction is to rise and vice versa. The difference between the two prices is recorded as volume (rounded). A set of buy and sell logic can be set based on the buy and sell signals and spreads: if a buy signal is given and the current account is long or open, then the contract with the corresponding volume units is bought; if it is short, then a certain percentage of the holding contract is sold. For sell signals, a reverse treatment using the same rules is sufficient.

In the event of a change in the main contract, the strategy empties the original contract holdings and buys the same number of new contracts. During the buying and selling process, trading-related fees and margin mechanisms are not taken into account due to the low trading frequency of the strategy. In addition, in order to better observe the accuracy of the buy and sell signals, no maximum position is set, taking into account the leverage effect of the margin system in the actual trading of futures.

3.3   Trading Strategies Based on LSTM

LSTM Model Setting. Since the input feature dimension is 1, the number of hidden layer units is set to 32. the length of the observation interval and the number of layers of the LSTM are used as hyperparameters, which are selected by the verification set effect. The loss function uses the most common mean square error for regression tasks [22] and the optimizer uses the RMSProp algorithm.

LSTM Experimental Analysis. Since in a practical quantitative strategy, the accuracy of predicting ups and downs as well as the accuracy of the price can affect its effectiveness. Therefore, two main indicators are used in evaluating the predicted outcome, the root mean square error and the F1 score.

Five sets of experiments were conducted based on the combination of different observation interval lengths P and number of layers L, and the performance of the indicators on the validation set was obtained (Table 3).

Table 3. LSTM validation set indicator statistics

Evaluation indicators	RMSE	F1 score	Precision	Recall
L = 1, P = 32	95.28	0.13	0.47	0.07
L = 1, P = 64	95.03	0.60	0.49	0.76
L = 1, P = 128	94.66	0.65	0.51	0.88
L = 1, P = 256	94.58	0.41	0.49	0.36
L = 3, P = 128	**94.51**	**0.68**	**0.52**	**0.98**

By analyzing the first four rows of data, it can be seen that LSTM can improve the prediction results with a limited lengthening of the observation interval length, but if the observation sequence is too long, it will affect the prediction results. At the same time, increasing the number of layers of LSTM is helpful for the model, but the gap is not significant.

Considering the larger number of participants in the multilayered LSTM model, this paper continues to include the comparison of pre-training (Table 4).

Table 4. Comparison of pre-training effects at L = 3, P = 128

Evaluation indicators	RMSE	F1 score	Precision	Recall
No pre-training	**94.51**	0.682	0.522	0.98
With pre-training	94.97	**0.688**	**0.524**	**1.0**

It can be seen that the addition of pre-training has little effect on the model.

Finally, a 3-layer no-pre-training model with an observation interval of 128 was finally selected as the best model to use for the test set (Table 5).

Table 5. LSTM test set indicator statistics

Evaluation indicators	RMSE	F1 score	Precision	Recall
LSTM	173.19	0.57	0.54	0.62

3.4   Trading Strategies Based on wLSTM

Modelling. The model used in this section is a wLSTM combining wavelet transform and LSTM model which requires a larger space to store information, so the hidden layer unit is set to 64, which is experimentally proven to improve the performance of the model. The model uses several different single-layer LSTMs to process the generated sequences separately. The required hyperparameters are the observed interval length P (32 or 128), the number of transformations D (2 or 3) and whether pre-training X is required.

Experimental Analysis. Based on different combinations of parameters, five sets of experiments were finally conducted and their performance on various indicators on the validation set was obtained. From the first four rows of Table 6, it can be observed that increasing the length of the observation sequence significantly increases the prediction error of the model, and the addition of pre-training is helpful for the model, especially for models with longer observation intervals. For the better performing third model, adding a transformation will get worse results, considering that the observed interval length is only 32, so too much decomposition will not get more trend information, but will increase noise.

Table 6. wLSTM validation set indicator statistics

Evaluation indicators	RMSE	F1 score	Precision	Recall
D = 2, P = 32, X = False	97.84	0.67	0.53	0.92
D = 2, P = 32, X = True	**96.24**	**0.68**	**0.53**	**0.97**
D = 2, P = 128, X = False	137.19	0.61	0.57	0.0.65
D = 2, P = 128, X = True	107.55	0.64	0.52	0.84
D = 3, P = 32, X = True	97.58	0.67	0.52	0.94

Synthesizing these analyses, the twice-decomposed pre-training model with an observation interval of 32 was finally selected as the best model to be used for the test set (Table 7).

Table 7. wLSTM test set indicator statistics

Evaluation indicators	RMSE	F1 score	Precision	Recall
wLSTM	176.94	0.67	0.55	0.85

3.5   Trading Strategies with Attention Mechanisms

Attentive LSTM. According to the previous experimental results, the LSTM model used in this section adopts a 3-layer unidirectional LSTM with an observation interval length of 128 and the remaining parameter settings remain unchanged. In addition, due to the higher demand of the attention mechanism for training data volume, three different training methods were used in the model (Table 8).

Table 8. Attention+LSTM validation set indicator statistics

Evaluation indicators	RMSE	F1 score	Precision	Recall
No pre-training	159.54	0.52	0.55	0.49
Pre-training (Al & Rb)	98.48	**0.68**	**0.52**	**0.99**
Pre-training (all)	**94.65**	**0.68**	**0.52**	0.98

Three sets of experiments were eventually conducted according to different training methods. As can be seen, the performance of the model continues to improve as the amount of pre-training data increases, but considering that there are many contracts with very little correlation to copper contracts in the previous period, the improvement is limited, so no more irrelevant contract data is considered for pre-training.

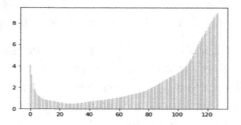

Fig. 3. Attention score

By obtaining the attention scores, we can observe the influence of the LSTM outputs on the results during the model prediction process. As can be seen in Fig. 3, the model mainly focuses on the later stages of the LSTM, but it also uses early stage information to make up for the omissions in the LSTM. Taken together, attentional mechanisms are helpful in capturing information.

Combining the above data, the model with an observation interval of 128 (based on all contractual pre-training from the previous period) was finally selected as the best model to be used in the test set (Table 9).

Table 9. Attention+LSTM test set indicator statistics

Evaluation indicators	RMSE	F1 score	Precision	Recall
Attention+LSTM	177.50	0.60	0.52	0.71

Transformer Model. The number of attention heads in the original paper was 8 and the number of layers was 6. According to Elena Voita et al. [23], an appropriate reduction in the number of attention heads in a machine translation task does not affect the effect and may even improve the effect. Therefore, attempts were made here to use 2, 4, 8 attentional heads, and 1, 2, 3 layers respectively. In addition, the observation interval was set at 128, all pre-trained using full data. Following the remaining settings, the experimental results are given by Table 10.

Table 10. Transformer validation set indicator statistics

Evaluation indicators	RMSE	F1 score	Precision	Recall
$n_{head} = 8, n_{layer} = 1$	95.72	**0.68**	0.52	**0.99**
$n_{head} = 4, n_{layer} = 1$	95.06	0.64	0.51	0.86
$n_{head} = 4, n_{layer} = 2$	**93.93**	**0.68**	**0.54**	0.90
$n_{head} = 4, n_{layer} = 3$	96.57	0.64	0.51	0.84
$n_{head} = 2, n_{layer} = 2$	94.38	0.65	0.53	0.82

From the first two rows, it can be seen that the reduction in the number of heads does not effect the results, while the number of parameters is much reduced. The number of layers derived from 2 to 4 rows is not as high as it should be, and needs to match the amount of data. And the last line can see that the effect of 2 attention heads is reduced compared to 4 attention heads. Further, the attention distribution of each head of the model at $n_{head} = 4$, $n_{layer} = 2$ was visualized by the Fig. 4 gives the four attention heads for each of the two layers. It can be seen that the pattern of capturing features is different between the two layers.

Fig. 4. Visualization of attention scores

Taken together, the model of $n_{head} = 4$, $n_{layer} = 2$ was chosen (Table 11).

Table 11. Transformer test set indicator statistics

Evaluation indicators	RMSE	F1 score	Precision	Recall
Transformer	173.88	0.65	0.55	0.79

3.6   Summary

This chapter uses the model in practice for forecasting and trading strategies, and the final results are summarized in Table 12. It can be seen that a large gap in the RMSE does make a significant difference in the effectiveness of the strategy, but when this gap is within a certain range, the effectiveness of the strategy is no longer linked to the indicator alone, but to the specific market conditions. And there is no clear link between F1 score and strategy performance. In the task of time series forecasting based on closing price information, the performance of the methods is relatively similar and has not yet been able to achieve a significant increase in yield.

Table 12. Summary of strategy results

Evaluation indicators	Rate of return (%)	RMSE	F1 score
Market	−1.62	–	–
LSTM	**10.88**	**173.19**	0.57
wLSTM	8.13	176.94	**0.67**
Attention+LSTM	8.19	177.50	0.60
Transformer	6.46	173.88	0.65

It is worth noticing that an anomalous volatility point was last seen in the test range, which was a huge swing on February 3, the first working day after the Chinese New Year holiday, when it was hit by a special event, the epidemic, that could not be predicted from the index. Therefore, Table 13 shows the strategy indicators with the cut-off time at that point in time, which leads to a completely different conclusion from the previous one, where the yield has a certain correlation with the F1 score in the case of close RMSE.

Overall, the combined RMSE and F1 score provides a better measure of the effectiveness of a quantitative trading strategy based on time series predictions in the absence of a large external market shock, while after a shock, the results of the strategy become uncontrollable due to the misalignment of predictions.

Table 13. Summary of pre-shock strategy results

Evaluation indicators	Rate of return (%)	RMSE	F1 score
Market	2.43	–	–
LSTM	7.97	96.71	0.56
wLSTM	6.50	98.32	**0.68**
Attention+LSTM	9.64	97.28	0.62
Transformer	**12.39**	**96.23**	**0.68**

4 Conclusions and Prospects

This paper establishes a futures trading framework based on time-series forecasting that attempts statistical arbitrage by leveraging historical information about prices. For time series prediction, three different types of approaches are used, namely, LSTM with gate structures, wLSTM combining wavelet transformations with LSTM, and network structures that introduce attentional mechanisms (attention+LSTM, Transformer), all of which aim to obtain more information from long sequences.

Experiments show that the performance gap between the root mean square error of each method is small in the final prediction result, but due to the different characteristics of the network, there is a certain gap between the actual strategy effect, which can be reflected in the F1 score to some extent. In general, the best-performing Transformer model can achieve stable excess gains independent of market ups and downs through both long and short mechanisms. However, neural network models based on internal market information can appear uncontrollable when relatively rare external shocks that cannot be reflected in prices occur, leading to a certain loss of yield.

It can be found through experiments that the common root mean square error is not comprehensive for the measurement of prediction results, and the ability to distinguish between fitting and prediction is poor. More evaluation methods need to be combined, and the loss function and model evaluation function applicable to quantitative transactions can be further explored. In addition, unpredictable external information requires timely stop-loss and adjustment of the strategy, as well as the introduction of online information such as news to help the model make decisions.

References

1. Sezer, O.B., Gudelek, M.U., Ozbayoglu, A.M.: Financial time series forecasting with deep learning: a systematic literature review: 2005–2019. arXiv (2019)
2. Rumelhart, David E., Hinton, Geoffrey E., Williams, Ronald J.: Learning representations by back propagating errors. Nature **323**(6088), 533–536 (1986)

3. Bengio, Y.: Learning long-term dependencies with gradient descent is difficult. IEEE Trans Neural Netw. **5**, 157–166 (1994)
4. Hochreiter, S., Schmidhuber, J.: Long short-term memory. Neural Comput. **9**(8), 1735–1780 (1997)
5. Graves, A., Mohamed, A.R., Hinton, G.: Speech recognition with deep recurrent neural networks. In: 2013 IEEE International Conference on Acoustics, Speech and Signal Processing (2013)
6. Sutskever, I., Vinyals, O., Le, Q.V.: Sequence to sequence learning with neural networks. CoRR abs/1409.3215 (2014). http://arxiv.org/abs/1409.3215
7. Schuster, M., Paliwal, K.K.: Bidirectional recurrent neural networks. IEEE Trans. Signal Process. **45**(11), 2673–2681 (1997)
8. Graves, A., Schmidhuber, J.: Offline arabic handwriting recognition with multidimensional recurrent neural networks. In: Advances in Neural Information Processing Systems 21, Proceedings of the Twenty-Second Annual Conference on Neural Information Processing Systems, Vancouver, British Columbia, Canada, 8–11 December 2008 (2008)
9. Koutník, J., Greff, K., Gomez, F., et al.: A Clockwork RNN. Computer Science, pp. 1863–1871 (2014)
10. Chang, S., Zhang, Y., Han, W., et al.: Dilated recurrent neural networks (2017)
11. Cui, Z., Chen, W., Chen, Y.: Multi-scale convolutional neural networks for time series classification (2016)
12. Chung, J., Ahn, S., Bengio, Y.: Hierarchical multiscale recurrent neural networks (2016)
13. Zhang, L., Aggarwal, C., Qi, G.-J.: Stock price prediction via discovering multi-frequency trading patterns. In: Proceedings of the 23rd ACM SIGKDD International Conference on Knowledge Discovery and Data Mining-KDD 2017, ACM Press the 23rd ACM SIGKDD International Conference - Halifax, NS, Canada, 13–17 August 2017, pp. 2141–2149 (2017)
14. Wei, B., Yue, J., Rao, Y., et al.: A deep learning framework for financial time series using stacked autoencoders and long-short term memory. PLoS ONE **12**(7), e0180944 (2017)
15. Hui, L., Tian, H.Q., Pan, D.F., et al.: Forecasting models for wind speed using wavelet, wavelet packet, time series and Artificial Neural Networks. Appl. Energy **107**, 191–208 (2013)
16. Wang, J., Wang, Z., Li, J., et al.: Multilevel wavelet decomposition network for interpretable time series analysis (2018)
17. Mallat, S.G.: A theory for multiresolution signal decomposition: the wavelet representation. IEEE Trans. Pattern Anal. Mach. Intell. **11**(7), 674–693 (1989)
18. Bahdanau, D., Cho, K., Bengio, Y.: Neural machine translation by jointly learning to align and translate (2014)
19. Luong, T., Pham, H., Manning, C.D.: Effective approaches to attention-based neural machine translation. In: Proceedings of the 2015 Conference on Empirical Methods in Natural Language Processing. Lisbon, Portugal: Association for Computational Linguistics, September 2015, pp. 1412–1421. https://www.aclweb.org/anthology/D15-1166
20. Vaswani, A., Shazeer, N., Parmar, N., et al.: Attention is all you need (2017)
21. Li, S., Jin, X., Xuan, Y., et al.: Enhancing the locality and breaking the memory bottleneck of transformer on time series forecasting (2019)

22. Heaton, J., Goodfellow, I., Bengio, Y., Courville, A.: Deep learning. Genet. Program. Evolvable Mach. https://doi.org/10.1007/s10710-017-9314-z
23. Voita, E., Talbot, D., Moiseev, F., et al.: Analyzing multi-head self-attention: specialized heads do the heavy lifting, the rest can be pruned. In: Proceedings of the 57th Annual Meeting of the Association for Computational Linguistics (2019). http://dx.doi.org/10.18653/v1/p19-1580

Hierarchical Attention Network in Stock Prediction

Liming Huang[1], Hongfei Yan[1,3]([envelope]) [ORCID], Siping Ying[1] [ORCID], Yansong Li[1] [ORCID],
Rui Miao[1] [ORCID], Chong Chen[2] [ORCID], and Qi Su[1] [ORCID]

[1] Peking University, Beijing, People's Republic of China
{liminghuang.pku,yanhf,liyansong,miaorui,sukia}@pku.edu.cn,
spying0403@gmail.com
[2] Beijing Normal University, Beijing, People's Republic of China
chenchong@pku.edu.cn
[3] National Engineering Laboratory for Big Data Analysis and
Application Technology, Center for Big Data Research, Peking University,
Beijing, People's Republic of China

Abstract. To solve the stock prediction problem, we propose a deep
learning model base on a hierarchical attention network. Our model is
divided into two models. The first model is the article selection attention network that transfers the news into a low dimension vector. This
model could identify the important factors in the news that affect the
stock price. The second model is a time series attention network which
combines the output of the first model and the transaction data as input.
In this model, we could figure out the potential impact between different
dates and summarize the historical data to predict whether the stock
price will rise or fall. The most innovative concept in this paper is stock
encoding. The model learns the difference between each stock and make
predictions more accurate by using the stock encoding. The experimental
result shows that the model fully utilize text features and make better
predictions than related research papers.

Keywords: Stock prediction · Hierarchical attention network · Deep
learning

1 Introduction

The trend of stock price influences not only the amount of money in the investors'
account. It also changes the country's business policy. That is why everyone
wants to predict the stock price even it is nearly impossible and full of risk.

Stock price prediction refers to the behavior of predicting the direction and
possibility of future stock price movements by analyzing the historical information of the stock market. This article focuses on predicting the stock price will
rise or fall, which is a binary classification problem.

Supported by: NSFC Grant 61772044; MSTC Grant 2019YFC1521203: research, development and demonstration of key technologies for knowledge organization and services
for Antiques based on Knowledge Graph; Peking University Grant 2020ZD002.

© Springer Nature Switzerland AG 2020
Z. Dou et al. (Eds.): CCIR 2020, LNCS 12285, pp. 124–136, 2020.
https://doi.org/10.1007/978-3-030-56725-5_10

With the circulation of stocks, stock prices will generate a series of fluctuations. In each trading day, opening price, closing price, high price, low price, trading volume, trading value, and other data are usually used to summarize the price fluctuations of the day. And the transaction situation, in which the closing price is generally used to compare with the previous trading day, as a measure of the stock price rise or fall in the day.

Firstly, given the stock s and the trading day t, the rise or fall of stock each day is defined as follows:

$$y_t^s = \begin{Bmatrix} 0, close_t^s < close_{t-1}^s \\ 1, close_t^s > close_{t-1}^s \end{Bmatrix} \tag{1}$$

Where $close_t^s$ represents the closing price of stock s on trading day t. When the closing price of y_t^s on trading day t is higher than the previous trading day $t-1$, $y_t^s = 1$, indicating that the stock price of stock s on trading day t increases; Conversely, if the closing price is lower than or equal to the previous trading day, then $y_t^s = 0$, indicating that the stock price has fallen or remained flat.

In addition to the relevant data on the trading day, text information related to stock-related financial news, institutional research reports, etc. may be generated every day, which can be used to understand the current stock market or event information related to certain stocks. The transaction data of stock s on trading day t is P_t^s, and the related news information is D_t^s. The stock forecasting tasks studied in this paper are defined as follows:

Given a stock s and an arbitrary trading day t, given a historical time series of length T-1 $[t - T, ..., t - 1]$. Use the stock trading information $[P_{t-T}^s, ..., P_{t-1}^s]$ and related news texts $[D_{t-T}^s, ..., D_{t-1}^s]$ to predict the rise or fall of the closing price of stocks s on trading day $\widehat{y_t^s}$:

$$\widehat{y_t^s} = f([P_{t-T}^s, ..., P_{t-1}^s], [D_{t-T}^s, ..., D_{t-1}^s]) \tag{2}$$

There are many challenges in the stock prediction problem. For example, the difference between stocks makes it difficult for the model to predict multiple stocks at the same time; there are many external influence factors and it is difficult to comprehensively analyze by using text processing methods; the text corpus is too sparse, and so on. In response to these challenges, this paper proposes a hierarchical attention network based on comprehensive processing of stock-related news text and stock transaction data. The first model is the article selection attention network that used to perform multiple daily news texts. Summarize to obtain low-dimensional feature vectors, and then concatenate the feature vectors that correspond to the news text and transaction data. The second model is the multi-head attention mechanism and the regularized dot product attention network. We use it to process historical data and predict the rise or fall of stock prices.

2   Related Work

The early research of the stock prediction focused on historical price data. It assumes that stock price is stable [1]. However, the stock price is actually not stable and full of noise [2]. Because the data is not linear, RNN-based model becomes one of the most famous models in the stock prediction rather than regression model. In the latest research [3], Zhang et al. Proposed a stock prediction method based on a recurrent neural network variant SFM (State Frequency Memory) model [4] for stock price prediction problems at different time spans. The SFM model is based on the Fourier transform which combines state and frequency into a matrix and uses this to record information at different frequencies over a long span such as short-term high-frequency transactions or long-term low-frequency transactions, making it possible to analyze trade events.

Hierarchical attention network has become popular in recent years because it can handle different hierarchical features. Wang et al. use attention mechanism at both the word level and the sentence level [5]. It can also be used in stock prediction. Kim et al. use GNN based hierarchical graph attention network with relational data to predict the stock movement [6].

Textual information like news or financial report is sometimes more informative than stock price [7]. Therefore, how to make full use of information such as stock news to improve the performance of stock forecasting methods has always been a hot topic.

In order to convert stock-related financial text information into a form convenient for computer processing, it is usually used to quantify the text into a feature vector. Simple statistical methods were attempted in early research work to automate the analysis of text, but the results were modest [8]. For example, the bag-of-words model [9] counts the frequency of the appearance of words in the text, and represents the text as a collection of words accordingly. However, this model lacks information such as the order of the text and the logical relationship. With the emergence of Word2Vec [10], GloVe [11], etc., deep learning methods can effectively acquire a low-dimensional vector for words, and at the same time capture the similarity between words. These models provide a good choice for text feature extraction. Yang et al. proposed an interpretable text-driven stock prediction method [12]. In this model, a word vector model is used to represent related news texts, and the word vectors in each text are averaged as the final feature vector. Then use the subsequent deep neural network to analyze the input information, and finally perform binary classification prediction.

However, in the past related work, only one of text data or transaction data was basically used. The judgments made were often one-sided. Researchers began to try to comprehensively analyze text features and transaction data at the same time. Capturing the potential characteristics of the interaction between external factors and internal values. For example, Zeya et al. extracted news text features and historical price data respectively, and then used a recurrent neural network to perform time-series modeling [13]. They used this to make classified predictions of stock price changes. R. Akita et al.'s work in 2016 [14] also tried to use both news and stock prices as inputs in the model.

3   Methods

Inspired by multi-head attention mechanism [15] and hierarchical attention network [16], this paper proposes a stock forecasting model based on hierarchical multi-head attention network, which applies two different levels of attention network to the modeling of serialized news text information and time-series historical information, respectively. Think of stock prediction as a binary classification task.

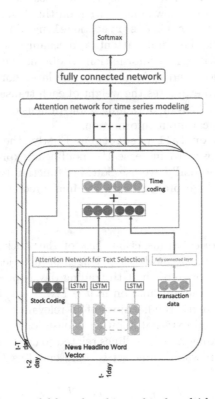

Fig. 1. Stock prediction model based on hierarchical multi-head attention network.

3.1   Framework

As shown in Fig. 1, the model proposed in this paper mainly includes the following five components:

- **Input layer**: Collect and process news headlines and stock trading data related to stocks in the past T days.

- Encoding layer: This layer mainly processes the daily input separately, and maps the daily news headline and transaction data into a low-dimensional feature vector representation, in addition to vector encoding the stock and trading day. Used to indicate the characteristics of each stock and to retain timing information for each historical trading day.
- Attention Network for Text Selection: This is the first level of attention network, which evaluates the relevance of the title text to the current stock through the attention mechanism, assigning higher attention weights to the more relevant text. Finally, get the low-dimensional vector representation after synthesizing all the news information on the day.
- Attention network for time series modeling: This is the second level of attention network. The multi-attention mechanism is used to process the feature sequences with time information to obtain the interaction between historical information, and then use one. The layer normalized dot product attention mechanism evaluates the weight of each transaction day's influence on the current time, thereby obtaining a low-dimensional feature vector that integrates all historical input information.
- Network for rise or fall prediction: Firstly, the multi-layer forward neural network is used to increase the nonlinear expression ability of the model as a whole. Secondly, we use SoftMax function to predict two classes, and the one with a high probability is the final prediction result

3.2 Input Layer

We use both the historical transaction data of the stock and the title of the relevant news as input in the model. The length of historical time we used is T, that is, when the stock price of the t-th trading day is predicted to rise or fall, the input layer will use the information in $[t - T, ..., t - 1]$ as input.

In the case of news texts, the headings of all relevant news are used as input. This paper introduces an external knowledge base for expanding stock-related entity noun sets for finding news headlines related to each stock in the news data set. The daily related news headline set is represented as D_t^s, and the input set of the time period is:

$$\overrightarrow{D}_{t-T}^s = [D_{t-T}^s, ..., D_{t-1}^s] \tag{3}$$

In terms of transaction data, this article uses six indicators such as opening price, closing price, high price, low price, trading volume, and trading value. In this paper, the normalization of data is performed for each stock to eliminate the difference in numerical scale between different indicators and different stocks. After normalization, the input for each historical trading day is:

$$\overrightarrow{P}_{t-T}^s = [P_{t-T}^s, ..., P_{t-1}^s] \tag{4}$$

3.3 Coding Layer

This layer mainly encodes the following four parts: stock code, title, transaction data and transaction time, so as to obtain the feature vector representation of the relevant part in each historical trading day.

- `stock code`: The model will receive different stock inputs simultaneously and make predictions, and each stock has its own unique nature. Therefore, the vector with dimension d_s is used to learn its own feature vector Es for each stock, which helps the model to better distinguish and identify the characteristics of each stock.
- `title`: For each news headline entered, it is first encoded using the pre-trained Word2Vec [10] model and then processed using a Bi-LSTM neural network. Since the output of each step of the Bi-LSTM network already contains all the previous input information, only the last step of outputting h_t is used. The output of the forward sequences and reverse sequences are concatenated to obtain the low-dimensional vector features of each title:

$$titleEmbed = concat(\overrightarrow{h_l}, \overleftarrow{h_0}) \tag{5}$$

- `Transaction data`: We increase the linear expression ability of transaction data through a fully connected layer to obtain the feature vector PE_s^t.
- `Transaction time`: Considering that the model will follow the multi-head attention mechanism for timing modeling, Therefore, the position coding in [15] is introduced to encode each historical event to obtain TE_s^t.

3.4   Attention Network for Text Selection

Since there may be a lot of related news in one day, the importance of different news is not consistent. The model should not continue to pass noise from the news into subsequent models, causing unnecessary interference.

The first level of text selection attention network calculates the correlation between each news and the current forecasted stock, removes the noise of unimportant information, and extracts the factors that really affect the price rise or fall of the stock.

This layer is based on the general attention mechanism. The relationship between stock coding and news headlines are obtained through a trainable matrix W. The score of each news is:

$$score_i = E_s \cdot W \cdot titleEmbed_i \tag{6}$$

Finally, the weighted average of title embedding is the output TE_t^s:

$$TE_t^s = \frac{1}{N} \sum_{i=1}^{N} a_i \cdot titleEmbed_i \tag{7}$$

Where N is the number of daily news, and a_i is the weight distribution of news, which can be obtained by normalization as follows:

$$a_i = \frac{exp(score_i)}{\sum_{j=1}^{N} exp(score_j)} \tag{8}$$

In addition to removing interference from unimportant information, this layer can also set the score of the null input to zero, thereby avoiding the negative impact of sparse input on the model.

3.5   Attention Network for Time Series Modeling

As shown in Fig. 1, the input of this layer includes the low-dimensional feature vector of news, transaction information, and time information. The vector E_t^s input for each trading day is defined as follows:

$$E_t^s = concat(DE_t^s, PE_t^s) + TE_t^s \tag{9}$$

The dimensions of each input satisfy the following relationship:

$$d_{TE} = d_{DE} + d_{PE} \tag{10}$$

The time series modeling network is shown in Fig. 2. It includes a multi-head attention mechanism, a position-based feedforward neural network and a layer of normalized point product attention mechanism.

The multi-head attention mechanism can be considered as a multi-parallel form of multiple self-attention mechanisms, which is obtained by splicing the results of multiple self-attention mechanisms. By normalizing the feature vector E_t^s of each historical trading day with all $histMatrix_t^s = [E_{t-T}s, ..., E_{t-1}s]$:

$$MultiHead_t^s = MultiHead(E_t^s, histMatrix_t^s, histMatrix_t^s) \tag{11}$$

This mechanism allows global information to be retained for each output and captures potential interactions for better information processing. Due to the nature of its parallel computing, the model will be more efficient.

The forward neural network processes the output of each historical trading day separately, and is mainly used to increase the nonlinear fitting ability of the multi-head attention mechanism.

Finally, the normalized dot-product attention mechanism is similar to the text-selection attention network. By comparing the stock coding with the information of each historical trading day, we can get the current impact of each historical trading day, and then obtain the optimal feature information.

3.6   Stock Price Prediction Network

The task of this paper is to forecast the rise or fall of stock, so the final output is $\hat{y} \in R^2$. Each element is between [0, 1], indicating the probability of price rise or fall on that day. This paper uses the Softmax function to calculate the probability of the final binary classification.

The probability that the prediction of stock s classified as J when $(P_t^s)_j$ is the trading day t. In this paper, the maximum probability category is used as the final prediction result, so the prediction result of the model is as follows:

$$\hat{y}_t^s = max((P_t^s)_0, (P_t^s)_1) \tag{12}$$

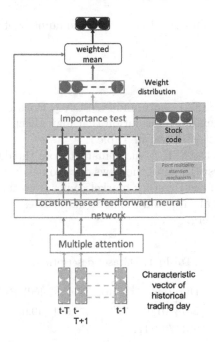

Fig. 2. Attention network for time series modeling

3.7   Model Parameter Learning

In order to obtain the parameters in the model, you first need to define the loss function of the model. Since the model uses the Softmax function for bi-class prediction, cross entropy is used as its loss function:

$$loss = -\sum_{i=1}^{N}\sum_{j=0}^{1} y_i^j ln(\widehat{y_i^j}) + a \left\| w \right\|_2^2 \tag{13}$$

Where $\left\| w \right\|_2^2$ is the L2 regular term, as a penalty term for the weight matrix in the network, avoiding the over-fitting problem of the model.

Based on the above loss function, this paper uses the Adam optimization algorithm [14] for model training. In order to ensure that the model can get a good result in the initial stage during training, firstly, the sample with more news data is used for training for a period of time. After the model is adjusted to a better state, all samples are used for subsequent training. Therefore, the problem that the loss of the initial training stage of the model is difficult to be reduced due to the text being too sparse is avoided

4   Experiments

We use Tensorflow [17] to train and test our model. The word vector dimension used in the model is 300, the stock coding dimension is 60, the news title length is 20, the historical trading angel is 14, and the number of units in each hidden layer is 256.

4.1   Dataset

Our dataset includes SSE A-share and NASDAQ. Both of which include stock transaction data and textual information that may affect stock price trends. An overview of the data set is shown in Table 1.

We use the data of the SSE A-share market from the dataset maintained by Zeya et al. In their thesis[13], and the news data comes from the Sohu Securities section. The data set of the US stock market comes from the data set maintained and opened by Ding et al. [18], and the news data comes from the financial pages of Reuters and Bloomberg.

Table 1. Dataset description.

Market	Duration	Shares	News	Fall/Rise ratio
SSE	2013/01/01 2015/09/17	772	78,381	49.9/50.1
NASDAQ	2006/10/10 2013/11/23	161	1,745	51.6/48.4

As can be seen in Table 1, the fall/rise ratio of the two data sets are evenly distributed. SSE A shares have a shorter time span, but the total sample size is significantly larger than that of the US stock market.

In order to make up for the sparse number of related news on each trading day, this paper refers to the work of Yang et al. [12], introduces an external knowledge base, and constructs a list of related entity nouns for each stock, thereby expanding the collection of related news.

4.2   Baseline Algorithms

In order to verify the validity of the model in this paper, some recent stock prediction methods based on deep learning neural network models are selected in this experiment to compare with this method:

– CNN-Static [19]: Text feature extraction and classification tasks using CNN.
– Price-SFM [4]: As one of the variants of the RNN, the Fourier transform is used to extract the transaction information of different frequencies in the historical trading of stocks to predict the stock price.
– Event-Embedding [18]: Structured events are extracted from news headlines, and low-dimensional vector representations of structured events are learned using tensors. Finally, CNN is used to process and make predictions.

- `Price+News-PMI` [13]: The PMI algorithm is used to extract the positive and negative characteristics of related news, and then it is stitched with the transaction data, and the RNN is used for time series modeling.
- `Hier-Attention`: Our method.

4.3 Experiment Result

This article studies the task of forecasting the rise or fall of stock prices, which is essentially a binary classification problem. Therefore, the index of the experimental evaluation adopts the accuracy rate of the classification method. For sample i, record the real price change category as y_i, and the model predicts the price change category as $\widehat{y}_i$. So for all n samples, the accuracy of the model is:

$$accuracy = \frac{1}{n} \sum_{i=1}^{N} 1 \cdot (\widehat{y}_i == y_i) \tag{14}$$

The performance of each research method on the two datasets is shown in Table 2. Since the interface used by Event-Embedding only supports English, the experimental method is not tested on the SSE A share dataset.

Table 2. Performance comparison of different methods on two benchmark datasets (accuracy).

Model	SSE	NASDAQ
CNN-Static	0.5342	0.5304
Price+News-PMI	0.5531	–
Price-SFM	0.5671	0.5266
Event-Embedding	–	0.5264
Hier-Attention	**0.5746**	**0.5638**

From the results in Table 2, it can be seen that the accuracy of the four methods in the SSE is between 0.53 and 0.58, and the accuracy in the US stock market is between 0.52 and 0.57. The reason why the accuracy rate of the SSE A-share market is generally higher than that of the U.S. stock market is that the SSE A-share news text corpus contains part of the research news corpus. The title is usually more targeted and it helps forecast future stock price fluctuations. The other reason is the data size of the SSE A-share market is significantly larger than that of the US stock market so the model training is more adequate.

The CNN-Satic method performed the worst in both sets of experiments because the method only used news text data from the previous day as input, but the text input in both data sets of the experiment was very sparse. As a result, most of the inputs in the experiment are empty, and the model is equivalent to randomly guessing the output, so the performance is not ideal.

The Price-SFM method only uses historical transaction data as input. Although it lacks analysis of external and influencing factors in the text, it still performs very well because of its special structure that can successfully capture trading events of different frequencies in time series modeling.

Price + News-PMI uses two types of data as input at the same time, which performs better than the CNN-Static method. However, because it only extracts its positive and negative characteristics for news text, it still loses a lot of information. In addition, the Price-SFM model in time series modeling has greater advantages in the stock prediction task than the LSTM network used by Price + News-PMI, so the overall performance of the Price-SFM model is better.

Hier-Attention (method of this article) uses a bidirectional LSTM network to obtain the low-dimensional vector representation of news, and uses the attention network to integrate multiple news on the same day, which can get more useful information from the text. In terms of time series modeling, the second-level attention network is used to comprehensively analyze historical transaction data and news features. The model can learn the interaction between different trading days and the scale of current impact from historical information. Therefore, the results of our model on both datasets have achieved the highest accuracy.

Comparing the performance of different methods on the two data sets, it can be seen that the accuracy of other research methods on the US stock data set is only about 52.5, which is significantly lower than the results in the SSE. Our method in two datasets has similar performance. It is proved that our method has robustness to different datasets and achieve good performance regardless of the quality and sparseness of stock-related news text. Therefore, the experimental results fully verify the superiority of the method in this paper over other research methods in the task of stock prediction.

5   Conclusion

This paper focuses on the application of deep learning and natural language processing technology in stock price prediction, and proposes a stock prediction method based on hierarchical attention network. Through two different levels of attention networks, the news text is analyzed and the historical information is time-series modeled, and the input information is better understood to make the best prediction results. And the introduction of stock vector coding in this article enables the model to learn the unique properties of each stock, so as to make more targeted prediction results by combining the characteristics of different stocks.

This article conducts comparative experiments on the SSE A-share market and the US stock market. First, in order to verify the effectiveness of the method proposed in this paper, multiple benchmark methods are set up for analysis and comparison, and the effectiveness of the method proposed in this paper is proved. Subsequently, this article is compared with other recent stock prediction research work. The test results show that the performance of this method is significantly better than other research methods, which proves that our method makes full and effective use of input information in text feature extraction and time series modeling, and the superiority of this method in the task of stock price prediction.

References

1. Kumar, D.A., Murugan, S.: Performance analysis of Indian stock market index using neural network time series model. In: 2013 International Conference on Pattern Recognition Informatics and Mobile Engineering (2013)
2. Si, Y.-W., Yin, J.: OBST-based segmentation approach to financial time series. Eng. Appl. Artif. Intell. **26**(10), 2581–2596 (2013)
3. Zhang, L., Aggarwal, C., Qi, G.-J.: Stock price prediction via discovering multi-frequency trading patterns. In: Proceedings of the 23rd ACM SIGKDD international conference on knowledge discovery and data mining (2017)
4. Hu, H., Qi, G.-J.: State-frequency memory recurrent neural networks. In: Proceedings of the 34th International Conference on Machine Learning, vol. 70 (2017)
5. Wang, T., Wan, X.: Hierarchical attention networks for sentence ordering. In: Proceedings of the AAAI Conference on Artificial Intelligence (2019)
6. Kim, R., So, C.H., Jeong, M., Lee, S., Kim, J., Kang, J.: HATS: a hierarchical graph attention network for stock movement prediction. arXiv preprint arXiv:1908.07999 (2019)
7. Ruiz, E.J., Hristidis, V., Castillo, C., Gionis, A., Jaimes, A.: Correlating financial time series with micro-blogging activity. In: Proceedings of the fifth ACM International Conference on Web Search and Data Mining (2012)
8. Brachman, R.J., Khabaza, T., Kloesgen, W., Piatetsky-Shapiro, G., Simoudis, E.: Mining business databases. Commun. ACM **39**(11), 42–48 (1996)
9. Harris, Z.S.: Distributional structure. Word **10**(2–3), 146–162 (1954)
10. Mikolov, T., Sutskever, I., Chen, K., Corrado, G.S., Dean, J.: Distributed representations of words and phrases and their compositionality. In: Advances in Neural Information Processing Systems (2013)
11. Pennington, J., Socher, R., Manning, C.D.: GloVe: global vectors for word representation. In: Proceedings of the 2014 Conference on Empirical Methods in Natural Language Processing (EMNLP) (2014)
12. Yang, L., et al.: Explainable text-driven neural network for stock prediction. In: 2018 5th IEEE International Conference on Cloud Computing and Intelligence Systems (CCIS) (2018)
13. Zhang, Z., Chen, W., Yan, H.: Stock prediction: a method based on extraction of news features and recurrent neural networks. arXiv preprint arXiv:1707.07585 (2017)
14. Akita, R., Yoshihara, A., Matsubara, T., Uehara, K.: Deep learning for stock prediction using numerical and textual information. In: 2016 IEEE/ACIS 15th International Conference on Computer and Information Science (ICIS) (2016)
15. Vaswani, A., et al.: Attention is all you need. In: Advances in Neural Information Processing Systems (2017)
16. Yang, Z., Yang, D., Dyer, C., He, X., Smola, A., Hovy, E.: Proceedings of the 2016 Conference of the North American Chapter of the Association for Computational Linguistics: Human Language Technologies (2016)
17. Abadi, M., et al.: TensorFlow: a system for large-scale machine learning. In: 12th Symposium on Operating Systems Design and Implementation, vol. 16 (2016)

18. Ding, X., Zhang, Y., Liu, T., Duan, J.: Using structured events to predict stock price movement: an empirical investigation. In: Proceedings of the 2014 Conference on Empirical Methods in Natural Language Processing (EMNLP) (2014)
19. Kim, Y.: Convolutional neural networks for sentence classification. arXiv preprint arXiv:1408.5882 (2014)

Online Topic Detection and Tracking System and Its Application on Stock Market in China

Yuefeng Lin$^{(\boxtimes)}$, Zhongchen Miao, Mengjun Ni, Hang Jiang, Chenyu Wang, Jian Gao, Jidong Lu, and Guangwei Shi

Innovation Lab, Shanghai Financial Futures Information Technology Co., Ltd., Shanghai, China
{linyf,miaozc,nimj,jianghang,wangcy1,gaojian,lujd,shigw}@cffex.com.cn

Abstract. Financial markets are very sensitive to emerging news related to stock because investors need to continuously monitor financial events when deciding buying and selling stocks. Tracking important events has done mostly using rule-based methods in the past, which is time-consuming in the face of huge online news data. To track this issue, in this paper, a novel document embedding technology based on TF-IDF and BERT incorporating online text cluster algorithm to form an automated event detection system is proposed. Embedding technology is first used to encode text to vectors and then an online text cluster algorithm - SinglePass is implemented to accomplish topic tracking. Experiment results show that the proposed algorithms can effectively detect and track online topics. In addition, both domestic and international events such as the outbreak of novel coronavirus (COVID-19) and Sino-U.S. trade war and their impact on capital market in China are analyzed, which demonstrate the practical and economic value of proposed system.

Keywords: Text cluster · Coronavirus · Topic detection · Document embedding

1 Introduction

With the rapid development of Internet, the amount of data have grown exponentially in the field of forum, websites and social networks. In the face of such huge data information, how to extract valuable info with large potential commercial value is very meaningful to investors and firms that can aid users to perceive market trends and also make valuable investment decisions. However, detecting and tracking topic from huge number of corpus is still a challenge [5,8].

For the financial information service, users hope that they can catch important events related to a firm that may have impact on stock market and analyze the causes and effects. In the financial portals, however there are some drawbacks compared to other fields. Firstly, the coverage of a stock is not much and news often belongs to different stocks and even mixed together. Second, massive

Z. Dou et al. (Eds.): CCIR 2020, LNCS 12285, pp. 137–148, 2020.
https://doi.org/10.1007/978-3-030-56725-5_11

similar and follow-up news about the same event published via different news media, online news are often reprinted that lead to duplication everywhere. Last but not least, the search result about financial news are not organized by topic or time. All the above issues make it hard to search stock related news and figure out which news is more important.

Our motivation of the paper is to build a practical online financial events detection system to track important news may affect stock market so that the investors may be aware of the price fluctuation. To better utilize the potential information contained in financial events, business analysis between important events like outbreak of COVID-19 and stock market is also investigated.

The main contribution of this study includes:

1. An automatic online text cluster algorithm is proposed to detect and track hot-spot in financial field without human intervention.
2. We utilized extracted business events to make a correlation analysis between trade war and Chinese stock market. It proves that important events could had a great impact on stock market. To our best knowledge, it has not been reported in the literature till now.
3. Compared with other text cluster algorithms reported in literature, the proposed methodology can be applied to Chinese text corpus in real-world application.

The rest of the paper is organized as follows. Section 2 we discuss the related works of topic detection and tracking. In Sect. 3, each component of the proposed text cluster algorithm is introduced. Section 4 we employ it to the online topic detection task and validate its effectiveness on news with annotated topic. In Sect. 5, the correlation between topic and stock market trend in China is analyzed. Section 6 concludes the paper and present future works.

2   Related Works

Since our paper focus on two main research issues, financial events recognition approaches and business event analysis. The major literature about this two areas are introduced.

Topic detection and tracking (TDT) is a kind of technology which can organize the news events into the news topics. A topic consists of many related news from the initial news story to the follow-up news story. It always contain two main tasks, firstly it is necessary to detect the existing topics from the previous news collection and then the online topic detection and tracking system is used to process news stream. Zhang Song [15] used the minimum distance and the average degree of aggregation to select the initial cluster center point. The number of clusters obtained by the CURE algorithm was taken as the K value. Bai et al. [1] proposed a method of tracking user relationship, which mapped the blog to the feature space, and then used the improved K-Means algorithm to perform binary clustering to track related topics. In recent years, with the development and popularity of topic models, the topic model LDA has also been frequently used in topic detection and tracking tasks. Wang and Zhang [13] used the LDA model to solve the initial cluster center selection problem in the K-Means algorithm. They used LDA to select the most important M topics in the text collection. Then preliminary clustering was performed so as to find the cluster center. Liu et al. [7] proposed LDA-K-means algorithm for topic discovery about food safety on network. They selected the topic probability distribution of documents to represent each document, and then used K-Means to cluster these documents to get the topics. Han et al. [4] use two kinds of document embedding- bag of words and doc2vec to represent documents for clustering. Recently, Reimers et al. [10] proposed a modification of the pretrained BERT network that use siamese and triplet network structures to derive semantically meaningful sentence embedding that can be compared using cosine-similarity, which laid foundation for using BERT for TDT. However, both K-means and LDA popular used in TDT need a predefined number of clusters and is not applied to real-world online Chinese topic tracking. While BERT-based embedding used for TDF is scarce until now.

In business event analysis, previous studies focused on correlation analysis between news event and stock markets. Nuij [9] combined news events and stock technical indicators to research changes in stock excess returns. Feuerriegel and Ratku [3] analyzed the impact of event topics in the news on the stock price. Also, Tafti [11] studied real-time relationships between chatter on Twitter and the stock trading volume of 96 firms listed in the NASDAQ 100 Index. In 2016, Kim et al. [6] used text processing to study social sentiment and its links to mobile phone-based trading in the KOSDAQ and KOSPI stock markets of the Korean Stock Exchange (KRX). However, the above research is about U.S. and Korean stock markets, which obviously have different characteristics, micro-structures and mechanism compared with Chinese stock market. Therefore, in our work, we focus on utilizing extracted financial events to analyze the impact of big events on market trend.

3   Proposed Method

At present, topic tracking mostly utilize LDA, Kmeans and their extension model. Both of them need to know the number of clusters in advance before using, so the real-time online news stream can not be realized based on these methods.

To tackle this issue, in this paper, the Chinese news data is first feed to prepossessing module including cleaning the data and cut the Chinese sentence into words. Then, we combine BERT, a state-of-art language pre-trained model and TF-IDF to encode each sentence into vectors. Finally, the online topic tracking task is carried out by using improved SinglePass text clustering method.

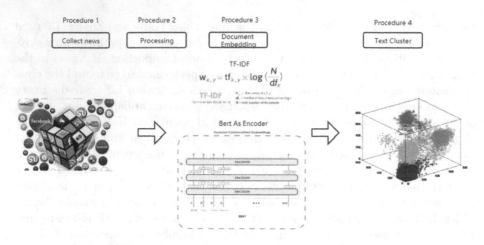

Fig. 1. Flowchart of proposed method for Topic Tracking

3.1 Algorithm Framework

The task of topic tracking is to group news related to same topic into one cluster and meanwhile take the degree of focus on the topic as the heat index. So it can provide a guideline for use of monitor and pre-warn for public opinion.

The basic steps of TDT is as follows:

1) Collect news data from different portal such as forum, websites using web-spider technology.
2) Using pre-processing technology to clean the original data by removing html tags and unnecessary information such as title, author using regex formula. Then we use Chinese character cut technology to cut each sentence into words for further processing.
3) Each sentence need to be tokenized by Vector Space Method (VSM) into tokens that can be recognized for computers.
4) Based on the distance between vectors encoded by VSM, cluster algorithms is used to calculate the nearest cluster each news belongs to.

In summary, step 1 provide the data resources, which is the foundation for further procedures. Step 2 and 3 that pre-process and document embedding is the necessary conversion components of TDT task. Step 4 the core components of TDT, the efficiency and precision of cluster algorithms is closely related to the effectiveness of topic tracking task.

The proposed algorithm framework is summarized in Fig. 1.

In step 3, the document embedding method used in our work contains TF-IDF and Bert as encoder. The introduction of them are present in the next section.

3.2 Document Embedding

In order to accomplish TDT task, Chinese characters in news need to be converted into tokens that computers can recognize, hence in this section we use embedding technology to learn the sentence-level information from texts.

First, before being converted into tokens, some necessary pre-process procedure is carried out as follows:

- Combine title and content part of news as a whole text
- Removal emoji characters and unwanted signs like '//', '@', ':-(' etc.
- Delete html tags in the texts.
- Using Chinese segmentation tool Jieba, all the texts are cut into Chinese phrases similar to English words. The segmentation rules are based on the default dictionary.

For the embedding technology for learning features from texts, TF-IDF is well-known for its simple theory and decent outcomes. Besides, BERT as a potent pre-trained contextualized sentence representation and has proven obvious improvement for many NLP tasks. In this work, both TF-IDF and BERT as text encoder is used for text representing learning. The introduction of them are listed as follows:

TF-IDF. TF-IDF stands for term frequency-inverse document frequency, and the TF-IDF weight is a weight often used in information retrieval and text mining. This weight is a statistical measure used to evaluate how important a word is to a document in a collection or corpus. The importance increases proportionally to the number of times a word appears in the document but is offset by the frequency of the word in the corpus.

BERT as Encoder. BERT uses a multi-layer Transformer encoder [12] to pre-train deep bidirectional representations by jointly conditioning on both left and right context across all layers [2].

Transformer makes use of self-attention (instead of RNNs or CNNs) as its basic computational block. Transformer uses a combination of self-attention and feed-forward layers in the encoder. In the standard Transformer model, the encoder is composed of a stack of 6 identical layers with each layer having two sub-layers, namely a multi-head self-attention mechanism and a position-wise fully connected feed-forward network. A residual connection is utilised around each sub-layer, followed by normalization layer.

For a given token, BERT's input representation is constructed by summing the corresponding token,segment, and position embedding. BERT is trained using two unsupervised prediction tasks, Masked Language Model and Next Sentence Prediction.

Benefit from large-scale pre-trained Chinese corpus, BERT-Base-Chinese [2] is used as an encoder for embed each news to fixed-dimension vectors. In our work, the form of news encoded by BERT is illustrated in Fig. 2. A [CLS] token and [SEP] token is inserted before and after each news respectively. Each news is encoded into vectors by BERT containing token, segment and position embedding together.

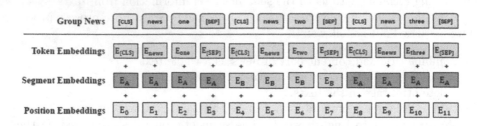

Fig. 2. Document embedding by BERT

Hybrid Method. TF-IDF and BERT has different advantages over learning features from texts. TF-IDF directly learn all the Chinese characters from the news while BERT may have words out of vocabulary for words not pre-trained on corpus especially in the field of finance. On the other hand, BERT can learn features from segment and position and have the advantage over TF-IDF by pre-trained on large-scale corpus in advance.

To combine their advantages together, in this section, we hybrid the vectors of TF-IDF and BERT jointly learned from texts together, which the firt half of vectors converted by TF-IDF and the other half obtained from Bert as encoder, the hybrid method is illustrated as follows:

$$Hybrid(w) = (\underbrace{w_1, w_2, ..., w_n}_{\text{TF-IDF}} \mid \underbrace{w_{n+1}, w_{n+2}, ..., w_m}_{\text{Bert}}) \tag{1}$$

3.3 Text Cluster Algorithm

Based on the text embedding technology introduced above, a classic online cluster algorithm named SinglePass [14] is used. Unlike other cluster algorithm such as Kmeans and DBSCAN that need to know the number of clusters K in advance, in topic tracking task, the hotspot is real-time with news stream, hence no predefined cluster number is known. Therefore, traditional offline cluster algorithm is not fit for online text cluster.

SinglePass algorithm processes the texts collections according to sequence and update the classes of cluster incrementally. It deals with one piece of news for one time. Before the text cluster task begins, it is required to be set a threshold T_c. If the similarity value between a piece of news in process and a existed topic cluster is bigger than T_c, the news would be classified into this topic cluster. Else, the system will create a new topic cluster based on this story and classified the story into the new created topic model. By adjusting the value of T_c, the system could control the granularity of clustering.

Combining the three diferent embedding technology TF-IDF, BERT and hybrid method with SinglePass algorithm, the TF-IDF-cluster, Bert-Cluster and Hybrid-cluster algorithm is proposed.

4   Algorithm Performance Validation

In this section, we evaluate our proposed topic tracking algorithm on financial news with annotated topic. First, dataset used in our experiments is introduced. Second, the well-used evaluation metric for TDT is present. Finally, we present our experimental result on metrics by comparing TF-IDF-cluster, Bert-Cluster and Hybrid-cluster algorithms.

4.1   Dataset

The dataset used in our experiment is collected by grabbing news from different financial portals. We annotate the topic of each piece of news related to finance published in January 3 in 2020 to perform online topic detection and tracking task. This annotated dataset contains 2790 news with 15 topics.

4.2   Evaluation Metric

In this paper, we adopt the traditional evaluation metrics which are widely used in clustering and information: Recall, Precision and F-measure.

According to the topic recognized by our proposed cluster algorithm and actual topic annotated manually, we simply modify precision, recall and F-measure calculated by following:

where n_i and n_j are the size of class i and cluster j, respectively. n_{ij} denotes the number of members of class i in cluster j. Then, the F-measure of cluster j and class i is defined by:

$$Precision i, j = \frac{n_{i,j}}{n_j} \tag{2}$$

$$Recall i, j = \frac{n_{i,j}}{n_j} \tag{3}$$

where n_i and n_j are the sizes of class i and cluster j respectively. $n_{i,j}$ denotes the number of members of class i in cluster j. Then, the F-measure of cluster j and class i is defined by:

$$Fi, j = \frac{2 * Recall i, j Precision i, j}{Recall i, j + Precision i, j} \tag{4}$$

F-measure of each class i is defined as

$$Fi = argmax(F(i, j)) \tag{5}$$

Similarly, the Precision and Recall of class i are defined as the corresponding values. We call Precision, Recall and F-measure of the class i: P_i, R_i and F_i respectively.

The global Precision, Recall and F-measure by calculating the weighted mean value for the corresponding metric as follows:

$$Precision = \sum_i \frac{n_i}{n} P_i \tag{6}$$

$$Recall = \sum_i \frac{n_i}{n} R_i \tag{7}$$

$$F = \sum_i \frac{n_i}{n} F_i \tag{8}$$

where n is the total number of topics in the corpus.

4.3   Experimental Results

The three algorithms on experimental results that text-representing method combined with SinglePass is summarized in Table 1.

Table 1. Performance comparison between three algorithms on dataset

	Precision	Recall	F-measure
TF-IDF	88.2%	92.1%	90.5%
Bert	91.2%	89.5%	90.3%
Hybrid	91.5%	92.3%	91.9%

It can be seen from Table 1 that for all three performance metric-precision, recall and F-measure, Hybrid performs the best, followed by Bert and TF-IDF. This finding means TF-IDF and BERT complements each other by converting sentences to vectors. Bert has the problem that out of vocabulary for words not pre-trained on corpus but has the advantage over TF-IDF that contains segment and position information.

5   Application

In this section, based on proposed event recognition system, we study the impact of events that may influence stock market in China. From 2019 to 2020, Sino-U.S. trade war and COVID-19 is the two most impressive event that has a great impact globally. First, we cluster relevant news related to these two topic by using embedding technology to validate the effectiveness of our proposed method. Finally we make a correlation analysis between stock market and these two events.

Visualization of Event Clustering Using PCA

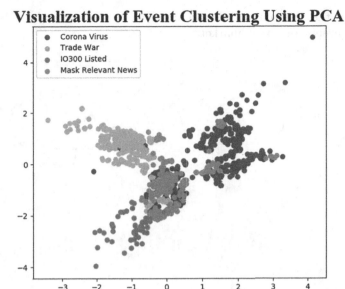

Fig. 3. Cluster results labelled by document embedding

5.1 Effectiveness of Document Embedding

In this section, in order to validate the effectiveness of proposed document embedding visually, we choose relevant news belongs to four important topics occurred recently. Besides COVID-19 and trade war, we also introduce some noisy event similar to these two topics. One is IO300, a tock index option listed (denoted as IO300 listed) and the other is mask relevant news. Figure 3 is the scatter plot of our document embedding results for four topics, which is reduced to 2D by using PCA from the original 300-dimension document embedding results. Each point represents one event belongs to a specific topic colored by different type.

It can be clearly seen that the points is divided into four groups. Some points belongs to topic-Mask relevant news is overlapped with COVID-19 because these news for two topics have similar words. From this perspective, the proposed document embedding can be used for topic detection task.

5.2 Correlation Analysis Between Events and Capital Market

Based on our proposed financial event recognition system mentioned above, our experimental procedure is as follows:

1) Using event cluster approach to classify online news stream into groups.
2) Find the cluster representing events and calculate the number of news as the topic heat.
3) Generate the topic heat trend of event and obtain SH index over time.

4) Calculate the Pearson correlation coefficient to observe the relationship between events and stock market.

Fig. 4. Market Trend of SSE and topic heat of trade war 2019.5.4–2019.12.31

Impact of Trade War on Stock Market Trend. For important events that occurred in year 2019, the Sino-American trade war is obviously an important event that has a great impact on stock market of both U.S. and China. Since 2018, President Trump impose punitive tariffs on Chinese products, and China also announced plans to impose tariffs on U.S.

SH index, published in 1991, is a weighted composite stock index with all the stocks listed on the Shanghai stock exchange, which represent the typical China stock market structure, provide an ideal sample to investigate China's stock market.

Because product tariff has a direct influence on import and export trade, closely related to stock market, our hypothesis is that topic heat of trade war has a negative correlation with SH index. To validate our hypothesis, SH index and topic heat of trade war is taken into consideration for analyzing stock trend based on events and also expand the utilization of our proposed event-recognition system.

As mentioned above, we plot the SH index and topic heat of trade war from 2019.5.4–2019.12.31 in Fig. 4. It can be seen from Fig. 4 that from the beginning the two curve trend of SH index and topic heat is just opposite each other. This means with the topic heat of trade war increases, the SH index drops accordingly.

For investors who wants to have a full-view about trade war, we list the important relevant news report along the topic heat about trade war detected by our proposed method. Then we organize the topic according to date in Fig. 4. From the event timeline and its relevant info shown in Fig. 4, we can basically have a idea about how the trade war evolve with time.

The coefficient between two trends reach −0.375. It validate our hypothesis that topic heat of trade war has a significant negative impact with SH index. The finding means stock market trend goes down with the debate about trade war upgrade online.

Fig. 5. Market trend of SSE and topic heat of coronavirus

Impact of COVID-19 on Stock Market Trend. For the other important event occurred in 2020, the novel COVID-19 is a global threat since it was identified in late 2019. Since the outbreak of COVID-19, equity markets in the EU and US dropped by as much as 30%. However, the correlation between coronavirus event and China stock market is still not clear.

We plot the SH index and topic heat of coronavirus in Fig. 5. The coefficient between them reaches −0.311 obtained by using Pearson correlation. The finding means coronavirus has a great negative impact on stock market.

6   Conclusion

In this paper, online text cluster algorithm with three different of document embedding is present, which is applied to the topic detection and tracking of real-world Chinese financial news. The experiment results show that our method performs well on the online detection and tracking of financial news, which the hybrid method that utilizing the advantages of BERT and TF-IDF shows the best performance.

Furthermore, we expand our event recognition system on business analysis by analyzing correlation between the topic heat of important event and SH index using Pearson correlation method. The finding is that important event may has a great impact on stock and future market in China. It gives extra information in terms of news for investors when deciding buying and selling stocks, which validate the practical and economic value of the system.

For future research on application side, it is necessary to expand our proposed of financial event-recognition system to more practical application like utilizing the hidden information from financial events to build a pre-warning system. Another possible direction is to track changes from all kinds of financial reports such as press releases and press about the company to gain insight to the development of a company.

Improvements to the methodology could be made to combine more state-of-art embedding technology to improve prediction accuracy. And compare the similarity not only the content of news but also ethology, location, time to enhance the performance of financial event recognition system.

References

1. Bai, W.Y., Zhang, C., Xu, K.F., Zhang, Z.M.: A self-adaptive microblog topic tracking method by user relationship. Tien Tzu Hsueh Pao/Acta Electronica Sinica **45**(6), 1375–1381 (2017)
2. Devlin, J., Chang, M.W., Lee, K., Toutanova, K.: BERT: pre-training of deep bidirectional transformers for language understanding. arXiv preprint arXiv:1810.04805 (2018)
3. Feuerriegel, S., Ratku, A., Neumann, D.: Analysis of how underlying topics in financial news affect stock prices using latent Dirichlet allocation. In: 2016 49th Hawaii International Conference on System Sciences (HICSS) (2016)
4. Kim, H.K., Kim, H., Cho, S.: Bag-of-concepts: comprehending document representation through clustering words in distributed representation (2016)
5. Hogenboom, F., Frasincar, F., Kaymak, U., De Jong, F., Caron, E.: A survey of event extraction methods from text for decision support systems. Decis. Support Syst. **85**, 12–22 (2016)
6. Kim, K., Lee, S.Y., Kauffman, R.J.: Social sentiment and stock trading via mobile phones. Association for Information Systems (2016)
7. Liu, J., Peng, Y., Zhang, L., Zhang, Y., Deng, J.: LDA-K-means algorithm of network food safety topic detection. Eng. J. Wuhan Univ. **50**(2), 307–310 (2017)
8. Nguyen, T.H., Cho, K., Grishman, R.: Joint event extraction via recurrent neural networks. In: Proceedings of the 2016 Conference of the North American Chapter of the Association for Computational Linguistics: Human Language Technologies, pp. 300–309 (2016)
9. Nuij, W., Milea, V., Hogenboom, F., Frasincar, F., Kaymak, U.: An automated framework for incorporating news into stock trading strategies. IEEE Trans. Knowl. Data Eng. **26**(4), 823–835 (2013)
10. Reimers, N., Gurevych, I.: Sentence-BERT: sentence embeddings using Siamese BERT-Networks. arXiv preprint arXiv:1908.10084 (2019)
11. Tafti, A., Zotti, R., Jank, W.: Real-time diffusion of information on Twitter and the financial markets. PloS one **11**(8), e0159226 (2016)
12. Vaswani, A., et al.: Attention is all you need. In: Advances in Neural Information Processing Systems, pp. 5998–6008 (2017)
13. Wang, C.I., Zhang, J.: Improved K-means algorithm based on latent Dirichlet allocation for text clustering. J. Comput. Appl. **34**(1), 249–254 (2014)
14. Xiaolin, Y., Xiao, Z., Nan, K., Fengchao, Z.: An improved single-pass clustering algorithm internet-oriented network topic detection. In: 2013 Fourth International Conference on Intelligent Control and Information Processing (ICICIP), pp. 560–564. IEEE (2013)
15. Zhang, Y., Song, A.: Application of improved algorithm based on K-means in microblog topic discovery. Comput. Syst. Appl. **25**(10), 308–311 (2016)

Semi-supervised Sentiment Analysis for Chinese Stock Texts in Scarce Labeled Data Scenario and Price Prediction

Ji Zhaoyan[1]([✉]), Yan Hongfei[1,3][iD], Ying Siping[1][iD], Chen Chong[2][iD], and Su Qi[1][iD]

[1] Peking University, Beijing, People's Republic of China
{zhaoyanji,yanhf,sukia}@pku.edu.cn,
spying@gmail.com
[2] Beijing Normal University, Beijing, China
chenchong@pku.edu.cn
[3] National Engineering Laboratory for Big Data Analysis and Application Technology, Center for Big Data Research, Peking University, Beijing, People's Republic of China

Abstract. The application of neural network in stock prediction is developing rapidly these years because of its excellency in series data processing. However, as most of research are conducted in English, data sources and labeled data are inadequate in Chinese. Especially for natural language processing tasks in specific domain where specialized labeled data are required to train models to adapt to terminology processing, specialized labeled Chinese in text data are very scarce, such as financial text data. To tackle this challenge, we proposed a semi-supervised learning method to generate well-labeled data and train BERT, a leading natural language processing model, to obtain a trained sentiment machine. Then we got stock-related text data sentiment score based on this machine and further combine the sentiment score and other transaction data as inputs for different neural networks to predict stock price. The experimental results on a large scale of Chinese stock data and texts showed that our proposed method successfully improved prediction accuracy compared to other established methods. Besides, we also examined our method's applicability combined with different neural networks when predicting different types of stock.

Keywords: Stock prediction · Sentiment analysis in scarce labeled data domain · Deep neural networks

1 Introduction

Stock market is an efficient way for companies to raise funds and for investors to generate financial returns. These advantages led stock market become a critical

Peking University Grant 2020: "New Ideas for Teaching 2.0" Key Project; MSTC Grant 2019YFC1521203: research, development and demonstration of key technologies for knowledge organization and services for Antiques based on Knowledge Graph; NSFC Grant 61772044.

© Springer Nature Switzerland AG 2020
Z. Dou et al. (Eds.): CCIR 2020, LNCS 12285, pp. 149–160, 2020.
https://doi.org/10.1007/978-3-030-56725-5_12

part of national economies. As stock becomes more and more inseparable to our life, precisely predicting stock price gradually draws scholars' attention. However, stock price changes in a volatile and chaotic way, resulting in dysfunction of lots of prediction methods. As deep neural network evolves and displays a extraordinary performance in times series data processing, it was frequently put into use in stock prediction tasks and generated relatively accurate results.

However, previous research was concentrated in English domain and lack of presence in Chinese, which caused the insufficiency of Chinese data source and labeled data accumulation. This problem becomes severely influential in natural language processing tasks in specific domain because specialized labeled data are needed for model training to identify and process terminology. Therefore, natural language processing related tasks in specific domain such as sentiment analysis faces a great challenge in Chinese. In this passage, we propose a semi-supervised learning method to tackle the problem of lack of Chinese labeled data in financial texts. We first crawled stock-related text data from a Chinese leading professional transaction website. We evaluated the sentiment score of those text data based on a naive sentiment model trained by general data. Then, we identified the ambiguous text with complex information and adjusted it manually. Based on this method, we successfully generated a batch of well-labeled data and further applied it into the fine-tuning of a leading NLP model, BERT, and managed to improve its performance in financial domain significantly.

In order to test this method's efficiency, we combined this sentiment analysis method into a stock prediction model in which we used sentiment score and transaction data to predict future close price for a certain stock. The specific problem can be defined as below:

Given a certain stock s and arbitrary trading day t, its close price can be predicted by a time series of its historical information of length T $[t - T, ..., t - 1]$. The information will include transaction data $[V_{t-T}^s, ..., V_{t-1}^s]$ and text data $[W_{t-T}^s, ..., W_{t-1}^s]$. The equation goes like below:

$$\hat{p}_t^s = f([V_{t-T}^s, ..., V_{t-1}^s], [W_{t-T}^s, ..., W_{t-1}^s]) \tag{1}$$

Following this definition, we combined the sentiment score with transaction data obtained from financial database and put them into prediction models. We used several neural networks as our prediction model to test our method's efficiency and performance characteristic on different neural network structure.

The experimental results further proved our method's efficiency and applicability in stock prediction field. Besides, it can generate different performance combined with different neural networks when predicting different type of stocks.

The rest of the paper will be organized as follows. Section 2 will introduce several related works. Section 3 will proceed with framework and details of our model. Section 4 will display the experimental results that directly show our method's efficiency. Section 5 will end with a conclusion of our work in this passage.

2   Related Works

Computer technology have long been adopted in stock prediction throughout its development history. After the birth of neural networks, the development of computer empowered stock prediction begin to accelerate. The neural networks show great excellency in series data processing which can be used both in stock transaction data processing and stock related text data analyzing. Based on financial domain knowledge, the stock prediction method can be categorized into three main segments.

The first segment is technical analysis driven prediction. This method believed market will repeat its behavior in a certain pattern. Therefore, they based their method on analyzing market data to discover the underlying patterns. The MACD [1] method, brought up by Gerald Appel, is a classical representation. They used stock's average price over different time span as an indicator to capture its future trend. Computer technology is, therefore, more adequate for this problem because of its superiority in handling data and capturing subtle trends. It made the first breakthrough after the application of auto-regression [2] model. Several scholars revised this model using machine learning techniques like SVM [3] to capture stock price's volatility. However, those methods still weren't able to capture the high volatility and chaotic. The neural network showed outstanding performance dealing those problem and therefore was put into use soon after its releasing. Among neural network frameworks, recurrent neural network displayed the highest capability [4] because its structure was specifically designed for time series data prediction. Later researchers have made several revisions on top of the RNN structure to make it more specific for stock prediction. Hu et al. [5] proposed a State-Frequency Memory network in a recent work. They added a Fourier Transformation in LSTM cells to distinguish long term and short term indicators for stock price trend.

The second segment is fundamental analysis driven prediction. This method based its prediction on the analysis of the intrinsic value of a company implied by its operating performance. The dependence of company inside information and unstructured analysis constraint computer technology performance as compared to human investors with abundant domain knowledge. But still, there are some researchers managed to find proxies for computer to discover insights using a computation method. Chen et al. [6] used mutual fund's portfolio data as a proxy for investment manger's stock preference. Their research proceeded with the assumption that stock held the same investor share same intrinsic properties, and therefore they were able to undermine inside information by leveraging public mutual fund portfolio data.

The third segment is information driven prediction. Text data such as news, announcements, and stock comments are used in this method to reveal stock's property and investors' sentiment. Neural networks are crucial to this method because it not only make precise prediction for time series data but also powerful in handling text data. Ding et al. [7] proposed a deep learning driven method to extract stock-related information from news and further predict stock price. Furthermore, neural network driven sentiment analysis can also be adopted into stock prediction by evaluating investors' sentiment through their comments because advanced financial research found out that investor sentiment can also affect stock price. Si et al. [8] have used comments extracted from tweets to derive sentiment score and used it to predict stock price. In later research, scholars used financial specific labeled data to train BERT [9], a state-of-the-art NLP technique, and obtained an outstanding performance in financial text sentiment analysis, successfully improving prediction accuracy.

However, as most of the research are conducted in English background, Chinese stock prediction research are relatively rare, especially the method based on sentiment analysis. The insufficiency of research results in the lack of accumulation of Chinese data source and labeled data, which obstruct future generation of scholars to deep dive into this area. Our passage proposed a method to generate labeled data in a semi-supervised way and solve the problem once and for all.

3   Method

Inspired by Dasgupta's method [10] of semi-supervised learning in scarce labeled data environment by categorizing data into groups and manually adjusting ambiguous group, we adopted a similar semi-supervised process to handle unlabeled text data for stocks. Then we generated labeled data and put them into BERT to obtain a well-established sentiment machine. We further derived sentiment score using this machine and combine the score with transaction data. Finally we run several neural network models with combined data as input to train prediction model. The overall framework is displayed below (Fig. 1).

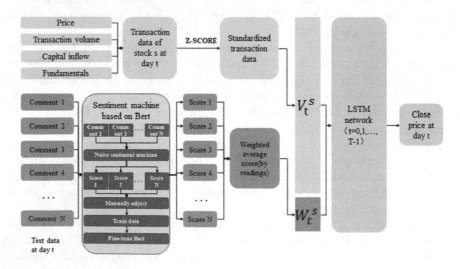

Fig. 1. Framework

3.1   Framework

As showed in the above framework, the proposed is model mainly composed of three layers:

- Text data processing layer: crawled data from a specific source to get abundant Chinese data sources. Trained the sentiment machine based on semi-supervised method to evaluate each texts and deliver their sentiment score.
- Transaction data processing layer: get four types of transaction data and standardized it to improve prediction performance.
- Prediction layer: adopted several neural network models to testify our method's efficiency and adaptability.

3.2   Text Data Processing

We used a leading Chinese online stock transaction platform Eastmoney as our text data sources. This website preserved lots of text information of company news and investor comments across a long time span as examples showed in Fig. 2. We applied a web-crawler technology here and a proxy IP tactic to successfully get 1.05M text data from 6 different stocks in each trading day between 2010 and 2020.

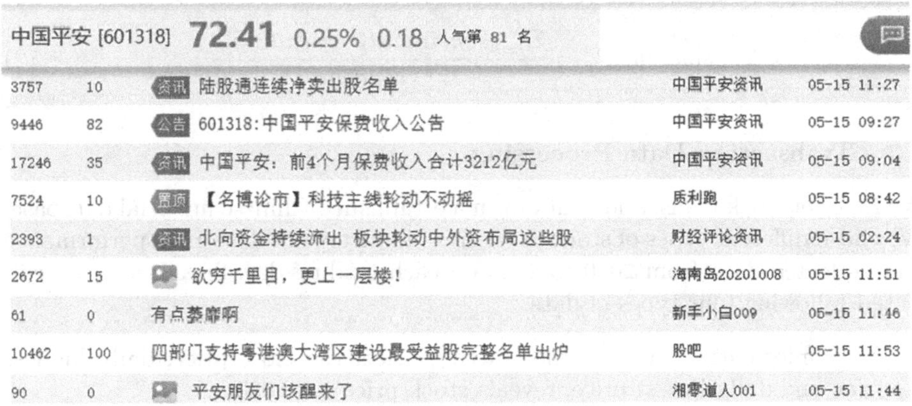

中国平安 [601318]	**72.41**	0.25%	0.18	人气第 81 名			
3757	10	资讯	陆股通连续净卖出股名单		中国平安资讯	05-15 11:27
9446	82	公告	601318:中国平安保费收入公告		中国平安资讯	05-15 09:27
17246	35	资讯	中国平安: 前4个月保费收入合计3212亿元		中国平安资讯	05-15 09:04
7524	10	股顶	【名博论市】科技主线轮动不动摇		质利跑	05-15 08:42
2393	1	资讯	北向资金持续流出 板块轮动中外资布局这些股		财经评论资讯	05-15 02:24
2672	15		欲穷千里目, 更上一层楼!		海南岛20201008	05-15 11:51
61	0		有点蔡廓啊		新手小白009	05-15 11:46
10462	100		四部门支持粤港澳大湾区建设最受益股完整名单出炉		股吧	05-15 11:53
90	0		平安朋友们该醒来了		湘零道人001	05-15 11:44

Fig. 2. Text data source

Then, we extract a batch of the raw text data as unlabeled train data. Firstly, we applied a naive sentiment machine trained on general Chinese data source mainly composed of comments from e-commerce website. Then we identified ambiguous text by matching raw data with stock terminology database. By this way, we filtered out a group of ambiguous text because of terminology. After manually adjusted, the ambiguous text's sentiment score became clear and qualified for being training data for the final sentiment machine. We combine the adjusted ambiguous group and the unambiguous group together to train BERT-Chinese model to obtain a accurate sentiment machine for stock comments and news. We tested the accuracy of the trained machine on testing data set and compared the result with the naive sentiment machine. The result in Table 1 shows our method significantly improved the sentiment analysis accuracy.

Table 1. Sentiment analysis accuracy comparison

Method	Accuracy
Trained BERT	88.2%
Naive sentiment machine	80.27%

Considered that different text have different level of influence on market sentiment, we adopted a weighted average method to calculate the sentiment score of a certain trading day t. Because the influence level of each text can be represented by its readings, which is recorded by the Eastmoeny website we chose. Therefore, we used the reading as weight to average the sentiment score of a certain trading day as showed in the following equation. We used all data (i = 1,2,...,N) of a certain day t to calculate the weighted average $sentiment_t^s$. Finally, we passed each trading day's sentiment score and reading to the prediction layer.

$$sentiment_i^s = \frac{\sum_{i=1}^{N} sentiment_t^{si} * reading_t^{si}}{\sum_{i=1}^{N} reading_t^{si}} \qquad (2)$$

3.3 Transaction Data Processing

We first get stock transaction data from a established Chinese financial database. We chose different types of stock in terms of industry and historical performance and collected data from 2010 to 2020 on each trading day. Specifically, we collected following four types of data:

- Price information: include the starting price, the close price, daily highest price and daily lowest price. reveals stock price's volatility.
- Volume information: include transaction volume, turnover rate and circulation market value. reveals investors transaction enthusiasm.
- Capital flow information: include net capital flow from mega size, large size, medium size and small size transaction. reveals different type of investors' different preference of holding a stock.
- Fundamental information: P/B and P/S ratio. reveals the stock corresponding company operating performance.

The distribution of those data is not united, highly likely to bring chaotic into prediction model. In order to eliminate the negative effect, we adopted Z-Score method to normalize all the input data. Z-Score is showed in the following equation. Then we passed all the normalized data together with data derived from text layer into prediction model.

$$normInput_i^s = \frac{Input_t^s - \overline{Input^s}}{\sigma_{Input^s}} \tag{3}$$

3.4   Prediction Layer

In this layer, we accepted data inputs from former layers and used them to predict future close price. We applied three different types of neural network to process the data to comprehensively test our method's efficiency.

– Multi-Layer Perceptron (MLP): this is the most classical neural network model. It is composed of input layer, hidden layer and output layer. Each layer is fully connected with multiple neural cells activated by non-linear function such as ReLU and sigmoid. Its forward propagation goes like following:

$$y_i = \sigma(\sum_i W_i x_i + b_i) \tag{4}$$

– Long Short Term Memory network (LSTM): this is a upgrade version of recurrent neural network. Introducing input, forget and output gates within each cell, LSTM successfully memorized crucial information from past time steps and used it to supplement current information. LSTM shows an outstanding performance in lots of series data processing fields and is therefore the most frequent used recurrent neural network.
– Gated Recurrent Unit (GRU): this is also a upgrade version of recurrent neural network. Similar to LSTM, GRU leverage reset and update gate to memorize past information. However, GRU's structure is simpler than LSTM, and thus easy to converge. Despite of convergence discrepancy, our experiments also discovered that they have different performance facing different type of stocks.

4   Experiments

We used Pytorch in Python to train and test our model. Our dataset and experiment results are showed below.

4.1   Dataset

To testify our method's efficiency on handling Chinese data, we obtained our experimental data from Chinese A share. We chose 6 different stocks with different market value, operating performance and industries to prove our method's adaptability across different stocks. We got their transaction data from 2010/01/01 to 2020/01/01 on each trading day through an established Chinese financial database Tushare. Then, we crawled the corresponding text data from Eastmoney website. The detailed information of those 6 stocks are shown below (Table 2).

Table 2. Stock information

Stock	Stock code	# days	# texts	Stock properties
Pingan	601318.SH	2431	337.9K	Finance, big size, high growth
Yili	600887.SH	2447	191.9K	Consumer, big size, stable
Wentai	600745.SH	1989	118.6K	Semi-conductor, medium size, volatile
Changjiang	600887.SH	2369	148.2K	Energy, medium size, cyclical
Yangquan	600348.SH	2477	117.7K	Chemical and Energy, small size, volatile
(ST)Gongxin	600701.SH	2160	142K	Manufacture, small size, poor performance

4.2 Experiment Setup

We adopted different neural network models stated above with different type of data as input. Specifically, we set up our experiment in 4 different ways:

- MLP + price data: we used past 30 days close price as input to pass into MLP model with 4 hidden layers and ReLU as activation function which is consistent with other RNN models.
- LSTM + transaction data: we used 14-dimension transaction data including price, transaction volume, capital flow and fundamental data. Then we used a LSTM network with a 30 days timestep to accord with MLP for comparison.
- GRU + transaction data: same input as the above LSTM model. We replaced the LSTM layer with GRU to compare their performance.
- LSTM + transaction data + text data: we used 16-dimension data combining transaction data and sentiment score and reading together to testify our method's efficiency.
- GRU + transaction data + text data: we replaced the above LSTM layer with GRU layer to expand our method's adaptability.

4.3 Evaluation Metric

In order to testify our method's efficiency, we introduced two way to examine the result and cross check with each other to comprehensively understand our experimental results. The first metric we used is Root Mean Square Error (RMSE) to evaluate the absolute distance between predicted result and real data. It is calculated as below:

$$RMSE(X, h) = \sqrt{\frac{1}{m} \sum_{i=1}^{m} (h(x_i) - y_i)^2} \tag{5}$$

The second way is to directly depict the figure of predicted and real data. By this way, we can visually understand the result revealed by RMSE.

4.4   Experiment Result

As introduced in the above section, we applied RMSE function as an evaluation metric. The detailed results are shown as below:

Table 3. Experiment result

Model	Pingan	Yili	Wentai	Changjiang	Yangquan	(ST)Gongxin
MLP	0.146	0.259	0.748	0.116	0.061	0.039
LSTM_data	0.148	0.145	0.819	0.098	0.018	0.116
GRU_data	0.206	0.099	0.825	0.064	0.021	0.050
LSTM_text+data	0.148	0.145	0.802	0.096	0.018	0.108
GRU_text+data	0.057	0.071	0.471	0.102	0.018	0.080

Based on this experiment result and together with some figure depicted from prediction result, we can derive following arguments:

- Our method showed significant efficiency over our experiments: Table 3 showed that RMSE decreased after we added sentiment data derived from our proposed method. The improvement was more obvious when combined with GRU model and applied to more volatile stock with higher growth potential. In order to gain a more comprehensive observation on our method, we put stock Pingan and Yili's result prediction figure below (Fig. 3, Fig. 4). As we can tell from the figure, the RMSE reduction came from more precisely fitting degree between prediction result and real data, especially on sections with high fluctuation. Our method is better at predicting future trend where the comparing method sometimes lagged behind.
- LSTM and GRU have different performance on different type of tasks: Through RMSE data, we can tell that those two networks don't have distinctive advantage over each other on whole scale. LSTM method performed better on high growth and fluctuate stocks such as Wentai and Pingan while GRU performed better on stable stocks such as Yili and Changjiang Electricity.
- MLP is invalid on stock prediction: Although MLP delivered lower RMSE result as shown in the table, Fig. 5 shows that it just averaged price over a certain time span. This methodology is ineffective in stock prediction field where even subtle trend can be crucial to capture.

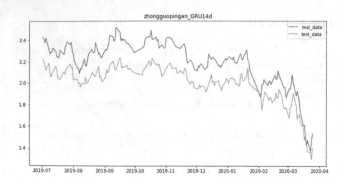

(a)Transaction data

(b)Extend text data

Fig. 3. Pingan's prediction result

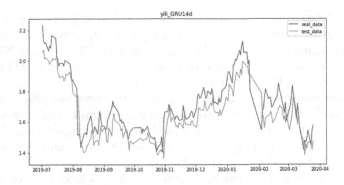

(c)Transaction data

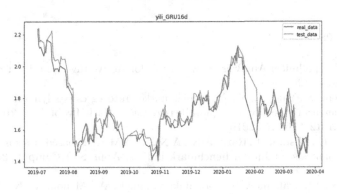

(d)Extend text data

Fig. 4. Yili's prediction result

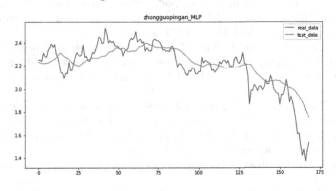

Fig. 5. MLP

5   Conclusion

Our paper focused on stock prediction problem on Chinese data. Specifically, we aimed to tackle a challenge lying on sentiment analysis in this problem, due to the lack of data source and labeled training data, which is a crucial part to train language processing model. We applied a semi-supervised learning method to generate training data and use the data to train BERT, a leading NLP model provided by Google. Based on this method, we successfully improved sentiment analysis efficiency on Chinese financial text data.

We further combined the sentiment data derived from our proposed method with stock transaction data and passed them into several neural network models to testify our method's efficiency when used into stock prediction problem. The experiment results successfully buttressed up our argument and also revealed its adaptability over different type of problems.

We believed our method can be widely used in this field as an effective way to supplement the insufficiency of labeled data and serve as a foundation for future works to generate more valuable insights.

References

1. Appel, G.: Technical Analysis: Power Tools for Active Investors. FT Press, Upper Saddle River (2005)
2. Li, L., Leng, S., Yang, J., Yu, M.: Stock market autoregressive dynamics: a multinational comparative study with quantile regression. Math. Probl. Eng. **2016**(PT.10), 1285768.1–1285768.15 (2016)
3. Nayak, R.K., Mishra, D., Rath, A.K.: A Naïve SVM-KNN based stock market trend reversal analysis for Indian benchmark indices. Appl. Soft Comput. **35**, 670–680 (2015)
4. Selvin, S., Vinayakumar, R., Gopalakrishnan, E. A., Menon, V. K., Soman, K. P.: Stock price prediction using LSTM, RNN and CNN-sliding window model. In: 2017 International Conference on Advances in Computing, Communications and Informatics (ICACCI), pp. 1643–1647 (2017)
5. Hu, H., Qi, G.-J.: State-frequency memory recurrent neural networks. In: Proceedings of the 34th International Conference on Machine Learning, Sydney, NSW, Australia, vol. 70, pp. 1568–1577 (2017). JMLR.org
6. Chen, C., Zhao, L., Bian, J., Xing, C., Liu, T.-Y.: Investment behaviors can tell what inside: exploring stock intrinsic properties for stock trend prediction. In: Proceedings of the 25th ACM SIGKDD International Conference on Knowledge Discovery & Data Mining, pp. 2376–2384 (2019)
7. Ding, X., Zhang, Y., Liu, T., Duan, J.: Deep learning for event-driven stock prediction. In: International Conference on Artificial Intelligence (2015)
8. Si, J., Mukherjee, A., Liu, B., Pan, J., Li, H.: Exploiting social relations and sentiment for stock prediction. In: EMNLP (2014)
9. Araci, D.: FinBERT: financial sentiment analysis with pre-trained language models (2019)
10. Dasgupta, S., Ng, V.: Mine the easy, classify the hard: a semi-supervised approach to automatic sentiment classification. In: ACL 2009, Proceedings of the 47th Annual Meeting of the Association for Computational Linguistics and the 4th International Joint Conference on Natural Language Processing of the AFNLP, 2–7 August 2009, Singapore (2017)

Author Index